BOTANY
PROJECTS FOR YOUNG SCIENTISTS

MAURICE BLEIFELD

BOTANY PROJECTS FOR YOUNG SCIENTISTS

PROJECTS FOR YOUNG SCIENTISTS

FRANKLIN WATTS
NEW YORK | CHICAGO | LONDON | TORONTO | SYDNEY

Cover photograph copyright © Jacob Mosser III/Positive Images

Photographs copyright © : Layne Kennedy: p. 14; Grant Heilman
Photography, Lititz, PA: pp. 17, 54 (Runk/Schoenberger); Photo
Researchers, Inc.: pp. 46, 80 (Jerome Wexler), 109 (Hugh Spencer/NAS),
111 (Dr. Jeremy Burgess/SPL), 126 (Mary M. Thacher), 130 (F. B. Grunzweig);
NASA: p. 64; Charles D. Winters: p. 105; Dr. Denis T. DuBay: p. 115; Barry S.
Kendler: p. 120.

Library of Congress Cataloging-in-Publication Data

Bleifeld, Maurice.
Botany projects for young scientists / Maurice Bleifeld.
p. cm. — (Projects for young scientists)
Includes bibliographical references and index.
Summary: A collection of activities and experiments involving
plants, exploring such areas as photosynthesis, plant structures,
and growth.
ISBN 0-531-11046-X
1. Botany—Experiments—Juvenile literature. [1. Botany—
Experiments. 2. Plants—Experiments. 3. Experiments.]
I. Series.
QK52.6.B54 1992
581'.078—dc20   91-43704 CIP AC

93-704

CONTENTS

Chapter 1
A Project for You
9

Chapter 2
Photosynthesis
16

Chapter 3
Plant Structures
31

Chapter 4
From Flower to Seed
48

Chapter 5
Growth and Development
59

Chapter 6
Heredity
90

Chapter 7
Ecology
107

Chapter 8
Out-of-Doors Projects
122

APPENDIX: Sources of Materials
135

Bibliography
137

Index
140

To my wife, Belle,
for her helping hand

1

A PROJECT
FOR YOU

A life-science project can be an exciting adventure in which you search out the secrets of living things. By means of a project, you can follow in the footsteps of scientists who have made important discoveries about how living things carry on their vital activities.

Botany projects deal with plants and can be interesting and challenging. Compared with animals, plants are relatively easy to grow and care for, and they are found almost everywhere—in the home, on lawns, and in gardens, parks, fields, woods, and vacant city lots.

Plants have various parts that can be experimented with to obtain answers to different questions about them: roots, stems, leaves, flowers, fruits, and seeds. Also, plants, like animals, carry on essential life activities such as digestion, respiration, circulation, excretion, reproduction, reaction to the environment, heredity, growth, maintenance of water balance, absorption, and osmosis. All of these lend themselves to projects of one kind or another.

Plants also carry on one activity that practically all living things on Earth depend on: They make their own food through the process of photosynthesis. All they need for this life-sustaining activity are water, light, and carbon dioxide. Knowing this, you could probably think of some ideas for projects to illustrate, control, or vary the conditions under which photosynthesis takes place.

For example: What is the best amount of carbon dioxide needed for photosynthesis to take place? What is the best intensity of light? Is the pH (or acidity) of water important?

Before going any further, you may wish to ask: What is a science project? How do I go about selecting a project to work on? What are the steps in doing a project? If I work on a project, how can I prepare it for a classroom assignment or science fair or for a competition like the Westinghouse Science Talent Search?

A science project may take many forms. Usually it is a scientific way of answering questions such as those mentioned earlier. To find the answer to such questions, you would start with a guess, known as a hypothesis, which might lead to a possible solution. Projects can also deal with the conditions under which one of the life activities takes place, with ecology, with heredity, or with hundreds of other topics.

Not all projects are experimental. There are also models, collections, and studies—for example, microscopic studies of plant parts. Although experimental science tends to be emphasized today as being the only "true" way of doing science, throughout history these other modes of scientific investigation have been pursued. Many botanists still work in the field—in the tropical rainforests, for instance—looking for new species of plants.

Generally, an experimental project is organized so that it includes a statement of the purpose of the activity; the plan of action (the method); the setup of the materials; the control; observations and a written record of all results; conclusions; and a record of your readings on the subject.

An experimental project usually has a control. This allows you to compare your experimental results with the results that occur under ordinary conditions. If you are trying to determine the effect of red light on plant growth, the control might be a similar plant exposed to ordinary light. If the red light causes any effect, the growth of the experimental plant and the control plant should differ noticeably.

To obtain materials for your project, you may want to speak to a science teacher. In some cases, you may need to order materials from a scientific supply company such as those listed in the Appendix of this book. Other sources are nearby colleges, research institutions, or industrial concerns.

You will find it useful to read as much as you can about the subject of your project. This will help broaden your understanding of the topic and provide you with information about the progress that scientists have made. Use the public library, school library, and nearby college libraries for magazines, books, and science journals to enlarge your background in the particular field.

CHOOSING A PROJECT

In choosing a project, you will want to decide on a topic that interests you enough so that you will be motivated to stick with it, even if it takes a lot of time or is difficult.

The projects in this book are meant to serve as a starting point in your search for a suitable project. One of them may suit you just fine in its current form. It may need to be modified. Or it may inspire you in a slightly different direction. Regardless of the way these projects motivate you, be sure to work under the supervision of a science teacher or other knowledgeable adult. This is especially important with projects involving chemicals or potentially hazardous techniques and if you are planning on modifying your project.

When you have finally decided on a project, be sure to discuss your plans with your science teacher or other knowledgeable adult. This person can review the directions and help you decide whether the project is a good one for you. The adult can also help you follow safety procedures and obtain materials. Certain equipment or procedures may simply turn out to be impractical in your situation.

WRITING THE REPORT

After you have completed your project, you should prepare a written report about it. In general, it should follow this arrangement:

A. Title Page: All capitals, title centered on the page, and your name, also centered.

B. Abstract: A separate sheet of paper containing no more than half a page, giving a short summary of the project. Include a brief statement of the problem, a sentence or two about your method, a short statement of the results, and a brief interpretation of these results. The abstract should probably be the last part of the report you write.

C. Introduction: A statement in detail about the problem you have selected. Include important background information to provide an understanding of the topic. If appropriate, mention a brief summary of research already done on the subject, and a statement of what your project will add to existing knowledge about the topic.

D. Methods and Materials: Describe your procedures in performing the project, mentioning apparatus used and details about time, temperature, light, and other important conditions involved. A labeled diagram or photograph may be useful in picturing the setup.

E. Results: This is where you summarize the results you obtained. You may include a drawing, graph, table, or photograph. Label these illustrations. Include a caption underneath, briefly stating what the illustration shows. However, if you use a table, you should place the caption above it.

F. Discussion: Give an interpretation of your results. You might compare your results with those of previous researchers. You may also want to include a statement of what the next logical step in the project should be. If you became aware of an error or weakness as you did the project, suggest a way of avoiding it the next time.

G. Summary: Give a brief statement of the conclusions you arrived at.

H. Bibliography: List the references you used and mentioned in your report. See the Bibliography at the end of this book for the typical format.

PARTICIPATING IN A SCIENCE FAIR

If you have ever attended a science fair, you were probably impressed by the great variety of projects and the orderly arrangement of each. Some projects are shown in Figure 1. These displays did not come about haphazardly but were well planned and thought through in advance.

To prepare your own display, first read the rules and entry requirements carefully. Then submit your application. Plan the layout within the amount of space allocated to you. Use neat lettering to center your title and subtitle. Display the main parts of your written report in an interesting and easily readable way that explains the story of the project.

Arrange graphs, tables, and photographs effectively to tell an observer your results in condensed fashion. If possible, include apparatus and materials to illustrate the setup. If you are questioned by judges or other people, try to give complete but brief answers. Refer to your written report for details not pictured in the display.

Figure 1 A botany project will fit
right in at a science fair.

SAFETY

"Better safe than sorry." This old saying applies to all types of work in science where living things are studied and experiments are conducted. Right now, and before doing any project, go over the following list of safety precautions. Also be sure to keep a lookout for the safety notes that are part of some projects.

1. Do your project under the supervision of a science teacher or other knowledgeable adult who can alert you to safety precautions.

2. Wear approved safety goggles when you work with chemicals. Also wear lab gloves and a lab apron.

3. Thoroughly rinse your hands with water after handling acids, bases, or other chemicals.

4. When using alcohol or any other flammable liquid, handle small quantities, provide for adequate ventilation, and keep away from a flame.

5. Learn the location of the nearest first-aid cabinet, fire extinguisher, and fire blanket.

6. When using a microscope, do not use the sun as a source of light.

7. Do not eat or chew leaves or twigs of plants, since even common plants like dieffenbachia, poinsettia, azalea, and hyacinth can be dangerous.

8. Do not wear contact lenses in the laboratory.

9. Avoid wearing loose clothing and long hair. They can be dangerous when you are using a flame.

10. When using electrical equipment, do not stand in a wet spot. Do not touch such equipment if your hands are wet.

11. Keep your work space neat.

12. When working in the field, always obtain permission before going onto private property.

2

PHOTOSYNTHESIS

Try to imagine what the earth would look like without any green plants. The landscape of such a scene would be quite bare—no forests, no fields, no farms, no parks, no lawns, no gardens. How about animals? There would be no herbivores like cattle, sheep, horses; they depend on green plants for food. No carnivores like lions, tigers, leopards; they feed on the herbivorous animals. No songbirds, no owls, no eagles; they depend either directly on green plants or indirectly on other living things that eat plants. For the same reason there would be no amphibians, fish, or reptiles. Do you think any human beings would be in such a picture? Is the scene shown in Figure 2 what you imagined?

Green plants are the basis of most life on earth because they contain chlorophyll, which acts as a natural factory. Chlorophyll absorbs energy from the sun and manufactures food by converting carbon dioxide and water into glucose through a complicated series of steps called photosynthesis. During this process, oxygen is given off as a by-product.

Figure 2 Can you see any plants or trees
in this landscape in Badwater, California?

The reaction taking place during photosynthesis can be stated as follows:

$$6CO_2 \ + \ 12H_2O \ \xrightarrow[\text{chlorophyll}]{\text{light}} \ C_6H_{12}O_6 \ + \ 6O_2 \ + \ 6H_2O$$

carbon   water   glucose oxygen water
dioxide

Safety note: Be sure to wear safety goggles, gloves, and a lab apron for all projects in this chapter.

CHLOROPHYLL AND LEAVES

Chlorophyll is the green substance that gives leaves their color. When analyzed, chlorophyll is found to be a mixture of several pigments: the green pigments chlorophyll *a* and chlorophyll *b*, and the orange pigment carotene and the yellow pigment xanthophyll, colors normally masked by the chlorophyll. In the fall, however, when leaves stop producing chlorophyll, these pigments become more prominent as leaves turn orange, yellow, and red.

Prepare a display of leaves to show their range of chlorophyll colors from very light green to very dark green. Include leaves that have more than one color, from plants such as coleus, pothos, and silver geranium. Is there any relationship between their shade of color and their environment or their exposure to sunlight?

SEPARATING THE PIGMENTS OF CHLOROPHYLL

Safety notes: Work under supervision. Wear safety goggles. Acetone and petroleum ether have strong fumes and are highly flammable. Work in a well-ventilated area, keep away from heat or flames, and avoid breathing the fumes.

Paper chromatography is a valuable technique for separating the pigments in chlorophyll. Follow these steps: With a mortar and pestle, grind two or three spinach leaves with a little sand and 5 milliliters (mL) of acetone. When the acetone has turned dark green, pour the extract into a small container and cover it to prevent evaporation.

Cut a strip of filter paper 20 centimeters (cm) long and 1.5 cm wide. Use a pipette to place a drop of the extract 1 cm from the end. When the drop has dried, add a second drop to the same spot. Repeat the procedure until you have placed 4 drops on the same spot, which should now be dark green.

Prepare a solution of 0.8 mL of acetone and 9.2 mL of petroleum ether. Pour this solution into a standard test tube to a depth of 1.5 cm. Slowly lower the strip of filter paper into the test tube until the spot of chlorophyll extract is just above the level of the solvent. Keep the filter paper from touching the sides of the test tube. Use a stopper to keep the strip in place. Hold the test tube upright in a test tube rack. See Figure 3.

Observe the chromatogram—the pattern of chromotography bands—formed as the solvent moves up along the strip of filter paper past the green spot of pigments. Remove the strip and let it dry. Do you see bands of color left by the solvent as it carried the various pigments up along the strip? At the upper end of the strip, look for the yellow bands of carotene and xanthophyll; lower down, look for the blue-green of chlorophyll *a*, and below that the yellow-green of chlorophyll *b*.

• Conduct a study comparing the chromatograms of spinach and geranium leaves. How are they similar? Different?

• In autumn, just before the leaves start to change color (if you live where they do change color), study the chromatograms of maple tree leaves day by day. Prepare an exhibit of the chromatograms placed next to each other and observe the width of the bands, especially those of chlorophyll *a* and *b*. What happens to these bands as the leaves begin to take on autumn coloration?

• Compare the pattern of chromatography bands of

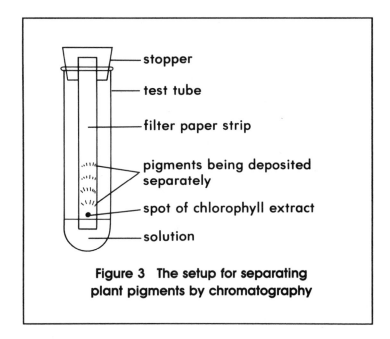

stopper

test tube

filter paper strip

pigments being deposited
separately

spot of chlorophyll extract

solution

**Figure 3 The setup for separating
plant pigments by chromatography**

maple leaves over a 2-week period in autumn with those
of other trees that exhibit different fall coloration, such as
oak, poplar, and linden.

• Some houseplants, such as philodendron, pothos,
and dieffenbachia, thrive indoors without any exposure to
sunlight. Other plants, such as geranium, begonia, and coleus, grow best in sunlight. Design a project to determine
if there is any difference in the chlorophyll of these indoor
and outdoor plants.

• Collect leaves of plants such as aster and ferns
growing in a dense forest where little sunlight filters down
to them. Prepare chromatograms of their chlorophyll. Are
they similar or different? Compare your chromatograms
with those of leaves of plants growing in a sunny field or
garden such as sunflowers, string beans, and daisies.

CHLOROPLASTS

Under a microscope, chlorophyll can be seen contained in tiny oval bodies called chloroplasts. To study chloroplasts, prepare a slide using a leaf from elodea (also called *Anacharis*), a plant commonly found in freshwater ponds. You can also obtain elodea at an aquarium supply store or pet shop. Since an elodea leaf is only two cells thick, you should be able to focus on a layer of cells, first under the low power of the microscope and then under the high power.

Turn the fine adjustment carefully until you can clearly see the many chloroplasts in each cell. You should be able to observe the chloroplasts moving around within the cells as they are carried along by the streaming cytoplasm. If at first the chloroplasts are not moving, you may have to wait until they get started.

• You may be able to hasten the streaming of the chloroplasts by warming the slide in your hand. Another method is to prepare the slide with a drop of warm water; determine the best temperature for this by using warm water of varying degrees—27°C, 30°C, 32°C, etc.

• Another way of stimulating the streaming action is to place the slide in sunlight. Keep a freshly made slide in the dark for half an hour. Bring it into the light and immediately examine it under the microscope to see if there is any streaming. Then place it in sunlight and time the length of exposure to sunlight needed for streaming to start.

• Determine the effect of artificial illumination on the start of the chloroplast movement. Use 25-, 40-, 60-, and 100-watt bulbs.

CARBOHYDRATE FORMATION

A green plant that carries on photosynthesis forms the simple sugar glucose, which is then changed to starch and stored in the leaves. The presence of starch in a leaf can be tested as follows.

Remove a leaf from a geranium plant exposed to light. Immerse the leaf in boiling water for a few seconds, remove it when it has become limp, and place it in a beaker of rubbing alcohol. Boil the alcohol gently on an electric hot plate for about 5 minutes. **Safety notes: Be careful not to spill any alcohol on the hot plate; it may start to burn. You can also boil the alcohol over a gas flame, but do so gently, as heated alcohol can start a fire.**

The hot alcohol will turn clear green as it dissolves out the chlorophyll of the leaf. Remove the leaf and rinse it with water. It should now be completely white. Spread it out on a flat dish and add iodine solution. Since iodine reacts with starch and turns it a blue-black color, the leaf will now become deeply stained, indicating that it contains starch. **Safety note: Iodine is toxic. Wash your hands carefully with water if you spill any on yourself.**

• Do all green leaves exposed to light store starch? Test the leaves of a variety of plants: houseplants, garden plants, leaves of trees, leaves of shrubs, and leaves of monocots (corn, lily, grass, tulip, hyacinth, etc.).

• If any leaves do not store starch, can you demonstrate the presence of simple sugar in them? Chop the leaf up into very small pieces and place them in a test tube half filled with water. Now add Benedict's solution and gently heat. If the blue color of the solution turns an orange color, it shows the presence of simple sugar. Prepare a list of plants that contain simple sugar but not starch in their leaves. **Safety note: Benedict's solution is mildly irritating to the skin. Wash your hands with water if you spill any on yourself.**

• Is the presence of chlorophyll necessary for the formation of starch? Obtain a silver-leaf geranium, a plant in which there is a narrow white border around the edge of each leaf. If there is no chlorophyll in the white border, will starch be present there?

Use alcohol to extract the chlorophyll from a leaf. After the leaf has turned completely white, can you distinguish between the border and the rest of the leaf? Add iodine to the leaf. Is there now a difference in appearance between the border and the rest of the leaf? What does this show?

• Make a study of other variegated leaves to determine if the nongreen parts store starch. Use plants such as coleus, dieffenbachia, and pothos and compare the results with the result obtained with the silver-leaf geranium.

CARBON DIOXIDE AND PHOTOSYNTHESIS

Is the rate of photosynthesis affected by the amount of carbon dioxide available to the plant? A water plant such as elodea is a simple and easily obtained plant for a project on this subject. Obtain a supply of elodea at an aquarium or pet shop.

Place several healthy strands in a very wide-mouthed jar (like a battery jar) of water that has stood overnight at room temperature. Cover the plants with a funnel whose tip is below the level of the water. Make sure the cut ends of the elodea point upward toward the neck of the funnel. Now fill a test tube with water and, keeping your thumb over the opening, lower it in place over the stem of the funnel. See Figure 4.

When you place this setup in sunlight, photosynthesis takes place and you can see bubbles of oxygen being produced by the plants. These bubbles begin to pass through the tip of the funnel into the test tube and collect at its upper end. When most of the water in the test tube has been forced out by the liberated oxygen, you can apply a simple test to prove that it is indeed oxygen. Light one end of a splint with a match and blow it out when it starts to burn. Now, while it is still glowing, insert the splint into the test tube. What happens to prove that it is oxygen? **Safety note: Since a burning splint can start a fire,**

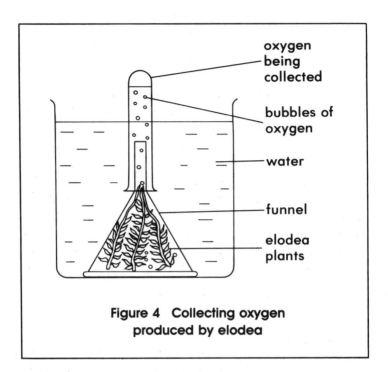

**Figure 4 Collecting oxygen
produced by elodea**

**put it under running water when you take it out of the
test tube.**

By measuring the length of time oxygen takes to displace 2.5 cm of water at the end of the test tube, you can conduct a project to compare the rate at which photosynthesis takes place with different amounts of carbon dioxide contained in the water.

• Prepare another battery jar setup of elodea. Use a soda straw to blow exhaled air into the water for 1 minute. The carbon dioxide contained in the exhaled air will dissolve in the water. Does the increased amount of carbon dioxide bring about an increase in the rate of photosynthesis?

• Compare with another source of carbon dioxide

dissolved in water: use a bottle of seltzer water to fill the battery jar and test tube. As you may know, seltzer water contains so much carbon dioxide under pressure that bubbles of carbon dioxide are given off when the bottle is opened. Could the relatively high concentration of carbon dioxide be toxic and reduce the rate of photosynthesis?

• You can supply CO_2 to the water by using a 0.25% solution of potassium bicarbonate, $KHCO_3$. Prepare this solution by placing 0.25 gram (g) of the chemical in a graduated cylinder and adding water up to the 100-mL level. How does the rate of photosynthesis of elodea in this solution compare with that in a control setup of ordinary water?

• Vary the amount of $KHCO_3$ by using such concentrations as 0.50%, 0.75%, and 1.00%. How is the rate of photosynthesis affected by each?

• Compare these results with those from using baking soda, $NaHCO_3$. Do the same concentrations yield the same results?

• Devise an experiment to determine the effects of a total absence of carbon dioxide on the rate of photosynthesis in elodea.

LIGHT AND PHOTOSYNTHESIS

Green plants carry on photosynthesis when chlorophyll absorbs light. Light provides energy for the series of steps in which glucose is formed from carbon dioxide and water and in which oxygen is given off as a by-product.

• How much exposure to light is needed before a geranium kept in the dark starts to carry on photosynthesis and begins storing starch? Keep a geranium plant in the dark for three days. Using the method previously described, test a leaf for the presence of starch. If no starch is present, place the plant in sunlight. Formulate a plan to test leaves at intervals of an hour to determine how long it takes for the plant to start storing starch. After you have gotten your results, should you repeat the activity? Why?

• Compare the results using other house plants. Make a list of "fast starch makers" and "slow starch makers."

• How is starch-making affected by exposing a geranium plant to continuous light from a 100-watt bulb for 24 hours a day? After 24 hours, test a leaf for the presence of starch. Continue testing at 4-hour intervals for the next 2 days. What do you conclude?

• What is the effect of using higher-intensity lighting: 200 watts, 500 watts, 1,000 watts? Compare with the effects of using just a 25-watt bulb.

• Determine the effectiveness of various periods of light on the production of oxygen by elodea. Set up an automatic timer in a dark closet or darkroom that will turn a 100-watt light on for 30 minutes. How much oxygen collects at the end of the test tube? Set the timer to turn the light on for 1, 2, 4, and 8 hours at a time. Measure the amount of oxygen produced at each exposure. Does it double when the length of time is doubled?

THE VISIBLE SPECTRUM

A prism can separate light into a display of its colors—red, orange, yellow, green, blue, violet—called the visible spectrum. You may have seen this effect in the sky when a rainbow is formed immediately after a rain shower; the water droplets in the air serve as prisms to the sun's rays.

The colors of the spectrum have different wavelengths, the shortest being violet and the longest red. Green plants appear green because chlorophyll reflects the green part of the spectrum and absorbs the other colors. Most absorption by chlorophyll takes place at the blue-violet and orange-red ends of the spectrum. The rate of photosynthesis is highest at these ends.

• Is photosynthesis affected by exposing plants to the

different colors of the spectrum? From sheets of cellophane of the different colors of the spectrum, construct large covers that fit over similar geranium plants that were kept in the dark overnight. Expose them all to sunlight for 4 hours. At the end of each hour, remove a leaf from each of the plants and perform the usual starch test. How do the results compare to one another? What control would you have to include to be sure of your results? Which color wavelengths are best utilized by the plants?

• Ultraviolet light has a shorter wavelength than the violet at the end of the visible spectrum. Test the effects of exposing plants to ultraviolet light. How will you avoid exposing your experiment to ordinary light? **Safety note: Ultraviolet light can damage your eyes. Be sure to wear the appropriate smoked goggles while using ultraviolet light.**

• Do different shades of a particular color differ in their effects on photosynthesis? Devise an experiment to find the answer, using as many shades of blue as possible, ranging from sky blue to navy blue. Do the same for red, ranging from pink to maroon.

• Make a study of the chlorophyll spectrum as seen through a spectroscope. **Safety notes: Work under supervision. Wear safety goggles and a lab apron. Acetone is highly flammable, so work in a well-ventilated area where no flame is present. It also has a strong, offensive odor, so avoid breathing the fumes.**

Prepare an extract of chlorophyll by grinding seven or eight leaves of spinach in a mortar with some washed sand and 50 mL of a mixture consisting of 40 mL of acetone and 10 mL of water. After the resulting mixture has become very green, filter it through filter paper.

Pour the filtrate into a test tube about 1 cm in diameter. Using a ringstand, hold the test tube in front of a bright light and observe it with a spectroscope. Study the chlorophyll spectrum and compare it with the standard spectrum in the spectroscope. Make a diagram, in color, of the absorption bands of the chlorophyll spectrum. Can you see which wavelengths of light the chlorophyll absorbs?

• Compare the chlorophyll spectrum of a common geranium with that of a plant growing out-of-doors such as a dandelion.

OXYGEN AS A BY-PRODUCT

A green plant that carries on photosynthesis gives off oxygen as a by-product. This is an important source of the oxygen in the air. A fish tank is usually stocked with green plants such as elodea to furnish oxygen to the fish. In return, the fish gives off carbon dioxide, which is used by the plant in photosynthesis. This oxygen–carbon dioxide cycle is an example of animal–plant interrelationship.

• Show how green plants are useful to fish. Early in the day, place six strands of elodea in a small aquarium containing a goldfish. Place another goldfish of the same size in a similar aquarium that has no elodea. Keep both aquaria near a window but not in direct sunlight. Why not? After an hour, observe the activities of the fish in each aquarium. Continue with your observations at hourly intervals until nightfall. Is there a difference in their activity? Continue with the project for the next two days or until you have to "rescue" one of the fish. Which one is rescued? Explain.

• How can the rate of oxygen production be measured? Prepare a setup in which you fill a battery jar three-quarters full of 0.25% solution of potassium bicarbonate. Stand a narrow bottle in it so that it becomes filled with the solution. Its top should be about 5 cm below the level of the liquid. Obtain a long strand of elodea and *carefully* cut its stem with a single-edged razor blade. Insert the elodea upside down into the bottle with its cut end extending 2 to 3 cm out of the bottle opening. Fill a test tube with the solution and, holding your thumb over the opening, lower it into the solution in the battery jar, with its opening

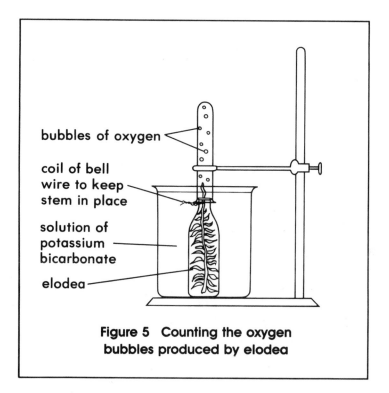

bubbles of oxygen

coil of bell
wire to keep
stem in place

solution of
potassium
bicarbonate

elodea

**Figure 5   Counting the oxygen
bubbles produced by elodea**

below the level of the liquid. Lower the mouth of the test
tube over the protruding end of the elodea stem. You may
find a small coil of bell wire useful in keeping the stem in
place. Use a ringstand to hold the test tube in place. See
Figure 5 for the setup.

Place a lamp with a 100-watt bulb 50 cm from the
setup. Place a container of cold water in between. Why?
Turn the light on for 5 minutes. If bubbles have begun to
stream up into the test tube, count the number of bubbles
produced each minute for a 5-minute period. What is the
average number of bubbles per minute?

Determine the number of bubbles produced at distances of 30 cm and 15 cm from the light. Record your

results on a table and plot a graph. How is the rate of oxygen production affected by the distance from the light?

Vary the intensity of light by using a 50-watt bulb. Is the rate of oxygen production now reduced by half? What are the results if you double the light intensity using two 100-watt bulbs? As the light intensity is increased, does the rate of oxygen production increase proportionately?

• Is there a limit to the intensity of light for photosynthesis to take place? Is there a decline in the rate of oxygen production if such a limit is reached?

• Do different wavelengths of light affect oxygen production? Which wavelengths, if any, are most effective? Least effective?

3

PLANT STRUCTURES

The bodies of most vascular green plants are made up of the following parts: *leaves,* which produce food by photosynthesis; the *stem,* which supports the main body of the plant and contains the vascular system through which materials are transported between the leaves and the roots; and *roots,* which absorb water and minerals from the soil and anchor the plant to the soil.

LEAVES

Leaves of different trees vary in size, shape, and arrangement. They may be very large (catalpa), long and narrow (willow), heart shaped (linden), triangular (poplar), oval (cherry), straight edged (dogwood), sawtooth edged (elm), deeply lobed (pin oak), star shaped (sweet gum), tulip shaped (tulip tree), mitten shaped (sassafras), fan shaped (gingko), or needle shaped (pine). They may be simple (maple) or compound (ailanthus).

  • Collect a variety of tree leaves. Keep them in a

plastic bag until you arrive home. A simple way to press and preserve them is to insert each leaf between the pages of a telephone book, then place six or seven heavy books on top. After 1 or 2 weeks in the book, the leaves will be dry and flat. Now attach each leaf to a sheet of white paper using narrow strips of self-sticking tabs. Place a neat label at the bottom of the sheet, giving the common name of the tree, its scientific name, and the place and date of the collection. If necessary, refer to a field guide to trees for the names of the trees. Prepare a display of the leaf collection under a title such as "Our Neighboring Trees" or "Trees in the Park."

• If your school has a plant press, arrange with your science teacher to use it to press the leaves more precisely. Or, you may wish to construct your own plant press using two plywood boards as covers, two long straps, and alternating layers of corrugated cardboard and sheets of blotting paper or newspapers. The overall dimensions should be about 45 cm × 34 cm.

• Experiment with the use of a microwave oven to press your leaves very quickly. In this project, you will be using a book in the microwave oven. **Do not allow the book to become too hot, since its pages may scorch or even catch fire.** Place a leaf in an old paperback book whose pages are not bound by metal staples (metal cannot be used safely in the microwave). Use a book that is no longer needed, since the heat of the microwave oven most probably will melt the glue that binds the book, and it will come apart. Line the bottom of the oven with a paper towel. Put another paper towel on top of the book. Add three to five dinner plates on top of that. Set the time at 1.5 minutes. After the microwave has stopped working, remove the book and leave the plates on top of it for about 15 minutes while it cools. Since microwave ovens vary in power, you will have to experiment with the best time.

• In the fall, when deciduous trees start to change color, prepare a display of as many leaves as possible, showing the range of colors from light yellow (birch) to deep red (oak).

• Perhaps your teacher can help you set up a "cross-country leaf exchange" with a student in a distant part of the country. Thus, if you live in the northeastern United States, you could press and mail a variety of leaves that have changed color to a pen pal in Arizona, for example, who is not familiar with the seasonal color phenomenon. In return, the other student could send you leaves of (nonprotected) native plants of that region. Your exchange of letters could describe the trees and could be part of a display on the subject.

• Since all the leaves of a particular tree have the same hereditary makeup, are they all identical in their appearance (as are human identical twins, which also have the same hereditary makeup)? Collect leaves from different locations on a low-growing tree. Include two leaves located on the outside of the tree, two leaves growing close to the trunk, and two leaves from in between. Also include two leaves from the southern exposure of the tree and two leaves from the northern exposure. Number the leaves with a small piece of masking tape to keep an appropriate record of their location.

Press the leaves. Trace each leaf on a sheet of graph paper, as shown in Figure 6. If the leaves have lobes, draw straight lines to connect the tips of the lobes. Count the number of squares on the graph paper within the lobe areas. Tabulate your results. Is there a difference in leaf size, shape, and lobe indentation? Summarize your results. What is a possible explanation?

• *Stomates* are the tiny openings in the epidermis of a leaf through which oxygen and water vapor are given off and carbon dioxide is taken in. To see stomates directly, obtain a begonia leaf and fold it sharply at an angle until it splits. Carefully peel back the outer skin, or epidermis, so that you can see it as a thin, colorless film. Place a small part of it on a slide in a drop of water and apply

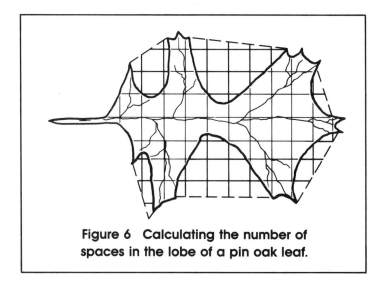

Figure 6 Calculating the number of spaces in the lobe of a pin oak leaf.

a coverslip. Examine the slide under the low power of a microscope and observe the stomates. Count the number of stomates in the field of vision. Compare the lower and upper epidermis of begonia in this way. Which has the larger number of stomates?

• Do most leaves have more stomates on their upper or lower epidermis? Make a study of a number of different types of leaves.

• Prepare a slide of stomates by using clear fingernail polish to paint a small area about 1 centimeter square on the lower epidermis of a begonia leaf. In a few minutes, after the polish has dried, press a strip of transparent cellophane tape firmly over the dried polish. When you peel the tape away, the dried polish containing an imprint of the microscopic stomates will be attached to it. Apply the tape to a microscope slide. No coverslip is needed. Observe the appearance of the stomates through a microscope. Compare the appearance of the stomates at different times of day and night. What do you conclude?

• Conduct a study of a number of outdoor and indoor plants in which you compare the times when stomates are open and closed throughout the day. Tabulate your results. What is your conclusion?

• Study the stomates of a cactus plant. (**Caution:** Handle very carefully if it has spines.) Are the stomates open or closed at night? During the day? Why?

• Observe the stomates of a begonia plant that has not been watered recently and whose soil is dry. Are the stomates open or closed? Compare with a freshly watered begonia. Does the availability of moisture influence whether stomates are open or closed?

• How many stomates are there in a square millimeter? With India ink, mark off a square millimeter on the lower epidermis of a begonia leaf. Prepare a slide with nail polish and use a microscope to count the number of stomates. Repeat the procedure for five different parts of the leaf and calculate the average number of stomates per square millimeter. Compare with other plants.

• How is a leaf affected when its stomates are blocked? Apply a layer of petroleum jelly to both surfaces of a geranium leaf. After 5 to 6 hours in bright sunlight, test the leaf for the presence of starch. Compare it with a control leaf. What are your observations? Explain the results.

• Devise a project to show the effect of polluted air in blocking the stomates of a plant with dust or other impurities.

• A plant that carries on transpiration gives off water vapor into the air through its stomates. This can be shown by attaching a strip of blue cobalt chloride paper to the lower side of a leaf on a geranium plant. (Cobalt chloride paper is blue when dry and pink when moist.) Does the cobalt chloride paper change color? If so, how long did this take to happen?

Which side of a leaf transpires more rapidly, the upper or lower? Attach a piece of blue cobalt chloride paper to each side of a leaf. Keep a record of the length of time needed for the papers to change color. Include a number of different plants in your survey, such as marigold, zinnia, bean, and begonia. Also include plants with vertical leaves, such as daffodil, tulip, corn, iris, and grass. Tabulate your results to show which plants transpire more rapidly: (a) from the lower surface, (b) from the upper surface, and (c) equally from both surfaces. Do these results show the relative number of stomates on the sides?

STEMS

Stems contain specialized tissue, called vascular bundles, which transports materials through the plant. The vascular bundles consist of two sets of tubes: *phloem tubes,* which carry food made by the leaves down to the lower parts of the stem and to the roots; and *xylem tubes,* through which water and minerals absorbed by the roots are carried up to the leaves. Stems may also store food for the plant.

A tree trunk has many branches through which the xylem and phloem tubes extend into the twigs and on into the veins of the leaves. During the summer, new buds are formed by the twigs in preparation for next year's leaves, stem growth, and flowers.

In winter, the following features can be seen on a twig (see Figure 7):

terminal bud (present in most trees) at the end of the twig;

lateral buds scattered below the terminal bud;

leaf scars, where the leaf petioles (stems) were previously attached to the twig;

vascular bundle scars (a row of dotlike structures in a leaf scar), which show the location of the vascular bundles that extended into the veins of the leaf;

bud scale scars (a series of rings encircling the twig a short distance below the terminal bud), which represent the place where the terminal bud of the previous year

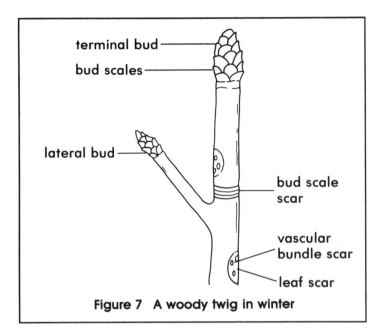

terminal bud

bud scales

lateral bud

bud scale scar

vascular bundle scar

leaf scar

Figure 7 A woody twig in winter

was attached and show the amount of growth since the previous growing season.

Buds of different trees vary in size, color, shape, and covering. They are usually protected by layers of overlapping scales.

• In the winter, make a collection of twigs from many different trees. Be sure to ask permission if any of the trees are on private property. *Carefully* use a knife to cut twigs about 20 to 25 cm long. Attach a piece of numbered masking tape to each twig and keep a record in a notebook of such data as place of collection, date, and special features of the tree. Look up the names of the trees in a guide to tree identification. Prepare a display of the twigs on a large poster board, labeling each with the common name, scientific name, and place and date of collection. The twigs may be fastened to the cardboard with wire twisted together on the back of the cardboard. Use a title for the display such as "Woody Twigs" or "Trees in Winter."

• Conduct a study on how winter twigs of various trees differ from one another. Compare such characteristics as size of terminal bud; shape of terminal bud; appearance of bud scales; arrangement of lateral buds (either opposite each other, alternating with each other or grouped together); distance between bud scale scars; shape of leaf scars; arrangement of bundle scars within a leaf scar (make a simple diagram); and other features (color of twig, presence of thorns, etc.).

• Speed up (force) the flowering of buds in the spring. During the winter, at weekly intervals starting in mid-February, cut a twig from a forsythia shrub that has many flower buds and place it in a tall jar of water. Keep it indoors in a warm place. How long do the buds take to bloom in each of the weekly samples? Does the process take less time after the beginning of March? If so, why?

• Conduct a study to determine the food-storing properties of various types of stems. In autumn, collect twigs of different deciduous trees such as oak and maple. Split each twig lengthwise and add iodine to test for the presence of starch. Why is this study suggested for the fall of the year? Tabulate your results in a chart listing the names of the trees and the results of the starch tests. Compare the results with a similar study in the spring. **Safety note: Iodine is toxic. If you get any on yourself, wash it off with water.**

• As a tree grows, a special group of cells in the stem called the cambium layer divides repeatedly to form woody tissue. In spring, when rainfall is plentiful, this growth is rapid and the woody cells are large in size and light in color. Later, in summer, growth is slower and the woody cells are smaller in size and darker in color. When a tree is cut down, a cross-section of the trunk shows layers of growth that alternate broad, light-colored rings with narrow, darker rings.

Study these rings in a tree stump. Count the number of dark rings to determine the age of the tree. Compare periods of rapid and slow growth. During which year in the life of the tree did most or least growth take place? If you knew when the tree was cut down, how could you use weather records in the library to determine the dates of rings when the weather was rainy or dry?

• Water and minerals are transported up through a stem from the roots to the leaves by means of xylem tubes. Study the rise of red ink in a jewelweed: The stem of this plant is almost transparent. Jewelweed usually grows near a pond or river, where the soil is quite wet. Dig up an entire plant, wash the roots clean of soil, and immerse them in a jar containing a solution of dilute red ink. Place in direct sunlight and observe the appearance of the stem and leaves every 15 minutes. Hold the stem against a bright light. Can you see the stained xylem tubes? Tabulate your observations. Explain the passage of the red ink throughout the plant. Cut a slice of the stem and observe it on a white background. Where is the red ink to be seen?

• Compare the rise of water containing red ink in celery stalks exposed to conditions in various places: in direct sunlight; in cool shade; inside a refrigerator; in warm water of varying degrees; directly in front of an electric fan set to slow speed, then high speed. Tabulate your observations. Explain any differences.

• Does water rise up the stem at the same speed in different plants? Devise a project using cuttings of such plants as celery, jewelweed, rhubarb, coleus, and bean. Make the cuttings close to the roots. They should all be of equal size, approximately 15 to 20 cm long. Use a separate container for each.

• A florist can dye a white carnation flower either red or blue by letting its stem stand in a solution of red ink or blue ink. Is it possible to color one white carnation flower with two different dyes? *Carefully* use a single-edged razor blade to slice the lower end of a white carnation stem vertically, exactly in half, up the stem for 8 to 10 cm. Spread the cut ends apart and immerse one in a jar of diluted red ink and the other in a jar of diluted blue ink. Support the main stem of the flower with a ringstand. See Figure 8. What are the results? How long did it take? How could you speed the results up? What other color combinations can you obtain?

ROOTS

The roots of a plant absorb water and minerals from the soil and anchor the plant in the soil. Some roots also store food originally manufactured in the leaves and then transported through the vascular system of the stem to the roots.

• How deep and wide does the fibrous root system of a plant extend? Conduct a study of a common weed (goldenrod, ragweed, etc.) in a vacant lot, where there would be no objections to your digging the plant up. Start your digging below the outermost leaves of the plant. Continue digging around the plant as deeply as necessary to remove the entire root structure with the attached soil. Measure the depth and width of the hole. Shake off as much of the soil as possible. Spread the plant out on a sheet of newspaper. Measure the length of the deepest and the widest parts of the roots. Describe the appearance of the roots. Compare the width of the branches of the plant with the width of the roots underneath. Is there a relationship?

• Continue your study of fibrous root systems with a number of other types of plants, including a grassy plant. Which has the deepest roots? The widest roots? Carry the plants home in a plastic container and spread them out to dry on sheets of newspaper. After a few days, gently shake the roots free of soil. Prepare a display, including the common and scientific names of the plants, and the date and place of collection.

• Some plants store food in an enlarged, thick root

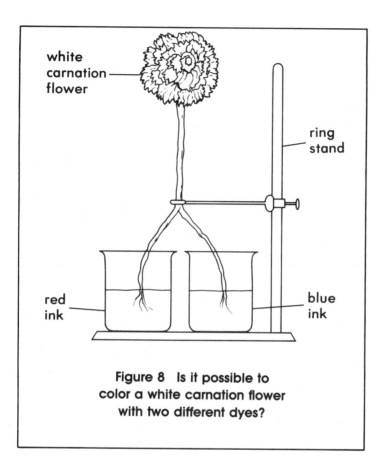

white
carnation
flower

ring
stand

red
ink

blue
ink

**Figure 8 Is it possible to
color a white carnation flower
with two different dyes?**

called a tap root. Set up a labeled display of different examples of tap roots such as carrots, radishes, sweet potatoes, beets, turnips, parsnips, and dandelions.

• Study the development of a root from a lima bean seed. Soak several beans overnight in a jar of water. Then, place them in a germination chamber formed by lining a jar with paper towel. Pack the inside of the jar loosely with newspaper. Fill the jar with water so that the papers become saturated and then pour off the excess water. Dis-

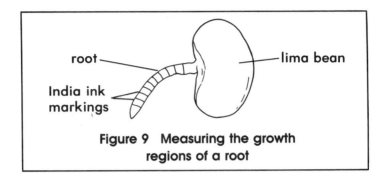

Figure 9 Measuring the growth regions of a root

root —

India ink markings —

— lima bean

tribute the lima beans so that they can be seen between the toweling and the side of the jar. As each bean absorbs water from the paper, it will sprout and send out a large root in a few days. Observe the appearance of the root. Can you make out its different growth regions?

• Determine the region of most rapid growth in a root. Start with five germinating lima bean seeds that have straight roots about 2 to 3 cm long. Carefully blot the root of a seedling with facial tissue and place it alongside a metric ruler. With India ink and a pen, gently draw lines at 2-mm intervals on the root, starting at the tip, as shown in Figure 9. Do the same for the other four roots. Cover a glass plate about 9 cm × 13 cm with paper towel. Arrange the seedlings on the glass plate and hold them in place tightly with a rubber band so that the entire length of each root is in contact with the paper. Stand the covered plate in a jar containing about 3 cm of water. Cover the jar with a glass plate to create a moist chamber. After 2 days, measure the distance between the ink lines on each root. Prepare an average of the length of each interval and record in a table like the one shown in Table 1. You can photocopy the page, but do not write in the book itself. Also plot your results on a graph. Where does most of the growth occur? How far back from the tip is this part of the

TABLE 1. REGION OF MOST RAPID ROOT GROWTH

Root Number	Length of Intervals (in mm)									
	1	2	3	4	5	6	7	8	9	10
1										
2										
3										
4										
5										
Total										
Average										

root, known as the region of elongation? Describe the appearance of other regions.

• Which part of a root binds to the soil? Plant tomato, radish, and bean seeds in separate paper cups containing a mixture of 50 percent potting soil and 50 percent vermiculite. When the plants have developed leaves, gently pull them up out of the soil. Examine their roots with a magnifying glass. Study the part of the root to which soil particles are attached. Are they fuzzy? This is the region containing the microscopic root hairs that absorb water and minerals and that are in close contact with the film of water around the soil particles.

• Since roots of plants bind the soil, what happens to an area when trees, grass, and other plants are removed?

Take a series of photographs of areas where erosion has occurred. Some places to investigate: a forest that was cut down; a slope bordering a new road cut where gullies have formed; a bare field without plants, exposed to blowing winds; a field overgrazed by goats, sheep, or cattle; the spread of a desert area. Prepare a display of your pictures under a title such as "The Loss of Plants Brings on Soil Erosion."

• Conduct a similar photographic survey and prepare a display on "How to Prevent Soil Erosion." Include pictures showing successful practices that preserve the growth of plants, encouraging the binding of the soil by their roots. Some ideas: forest conservation; planting of windbreaks; contour plowing; terracing; strip cropping; cover crops; crop rotation.

• Conduct a microscopic study of the rapidly dividing cells in the root tip of an onion. **Safety notes: Work under the supervision of a science teacher. Wear safety goggles, gloves, and a lab apron. Paradichlorobenzene has a strong odor, so work in a well-ventilated area. Paradichlorobenzene is toxic, and hydrochloric acid (although in a weak concentration) is toxic and corrosive. Wash your hands carefully with water if you spill any of these chemicals on yourself.**

Rest an onion bulb over a full jar of water so that its base is in contact with the water. If necessary, insert toothpicks around the onion to keep it in place, as shown in Figure 10a. When roots develop in a few days, cut off a tip about 1 cm long and soak it in a saturated solution of paradichlorobenzene for 3 hours in a cool place (12 to 16° C). Prepare a mixture consisting of 2% aceto-orcein solution (9 parts) and 1N hydrochloric acid solution (1 part).

Place the root tip and this mixture in a test tube and heat gently with a bunsen burner until it just starts to boil. Pour the contents into a small dish and cool for about 5 minutes. Remove the root tip with tweezers to a drop of 1% aceto-orcein solution on a clean slide. *Carefully* use a sharp razor blade to slice away the bottom 2 mm of the

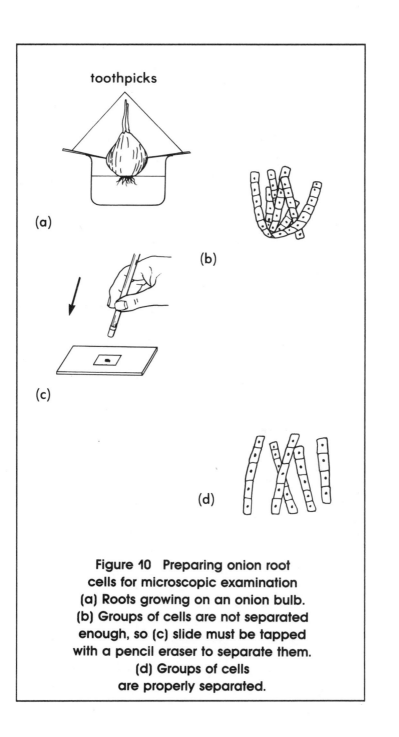

toothpicks

(a)

(b)

(c)

(d)

Figure 10   Preparing onion root
cells for microscopic examination
(a) Roots growing on an onion bulb.
(b) Groups of cells are not separated
enough, so (c) slide must be tapped
with a pencil eraser to separate them.
(d) Groups of cells
are properly separated.

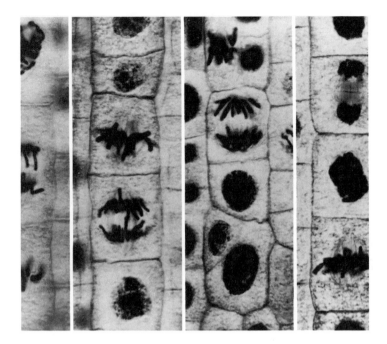

**Figure 11   Mitosis in
onion root tip cells**

root tip and discard the rest. Apply a coverslip and press
uniformly over the surface with the rubber eraser of a pencil to squash the root tip and spread it out. Apply filter
paper to the edge of the coverslip to absorb any excess
stain.

Examine the slide under high power to observe the
various stages of cell division and mitosis. If the groups of
cells are not properly separated (as shown in Figure 10b),
tap them with the pencil eraser (Figure 10c) until they appear like the cells shown in Figure 10d. Study the appearance of the chromosomes in each stage of mitosis: pro-
phase, metaphase, anaphase, and telophase. Count the

number of cells that can be seen in each phase. Compare with what you see in Figure 11.

• Will certain substances produce abnormalities in the chromosomes? Observe the effects of adding an aspirin to the jar of water used to germinate the onion roots. Compare with the effects of nicotine, coffee, and other substances.

4

FROM FLOWER TO SEED

The florist who uses the slogan "Say it with flowers" is advertising flowers as colorful and natural decorations. To the plant, however, flowers serve another purpose—they are essential for reproduction. Although flowers may vary in their brilliant colors, attractive fragrances, and particular shapes, they all have the same basic structures. Figure 12 shows these structures.

Flowers contain essential organs directly concerned with reproduction—*stamens* and *pistils.* The first step in plant sexual reproduction is pollination, the transfer of pollen from the *anther* of the stamen to the *stigma* of the pistil. A pollen grain that lands germinates a pollen tube that grows down the *style* to the *ovule.* Here, fertilization takes place and the ovule develops into a seed, while the surrounding *ovary* matures into a fruit.

Enclosing the stamens and pistils are the brightly colored *petals,* which often are very fragrant. Tiny glands at the base of the petals may produce sweet nectar, which attracts insects and hummingbirds that help in the process

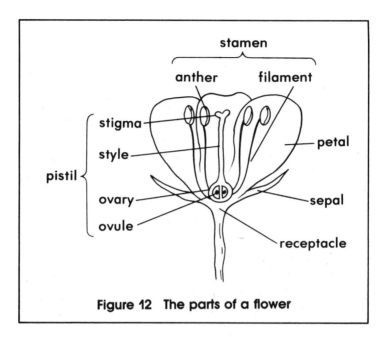

Figure 12　The parts of a flower

of pollination. Located outside of the petals are the *se-pals*—small, usually green, leaflike structures that at one time enclosed the flower bud. All of these parts of the flower are attached to and supported by a modified stem, the *receptacle.*

FLOWER STRUCTURES

Flowers may differ from one another in many ways. A flower that contains all of the typical structures (sepals, petals, stamens, and pistils) is known as a complete flower. By contrast, an incomplete flower has one or more of these parts missing. Flowers may also vary in the number and arrangement of the typical parts.

　• Conduct a study of a complete flower such as a gladiolus. A florist may be willing to donate flowers that are past their prime or that have not been sold. (**Note:** Do not pick flowers in a public park, or a nearby garden, without permission. Some wildflowers, too, are protected and cannot be picked at all.) Look for the typical parts. How many of each are there? With a razor blade, *carefully* cut the ovary in half down its length. With the aid of a magnifying glass, count the number of ovules. Prepare a labeled display of the flower parts on a poster board under the title "Parts of a Gladiolus Flower."

• Make a comparison of at least six complete flowers, such as petunia, azalea, rose, buttercup, apple blossom, sweet pea, and snapdragon. Prepare a chart like Table 2 listing the details for each flower. Do not write in the book itself.

• Study a number of incomplete flowers, that is, ones that lack a perianth (no petals and no sepals), have stamens but no pistils (staminate flowers only), or have pistils but no stamens (pistillate flowers only).

• Members of the aster family of flowers such as the daisy, sunflower, and zinnia contain so many small flowers massed together that they may be said to consist of a bouquet of flowers. Investigate the disk (center) flowers and ray (outside) flowers of a daisy. Are there stamens and pistils in each? If so, how many? Are they complete flowers? Are other structures present in the flower head? Compare with several other composite flowers, including dandelions and dahlias. Are disk or ray flowers present in all? Summarize your observations in a Comparative Chart of Composite Flowers.

• A corn plant has imperfect flowers. Staminate flowers are grouped in the tassel, at the top of the plant. Pistillate flowers are located further down. Separate out individual staminate flowers. How many anthers are there in each? Study individual pistillate flowers. How long is the style and where is it attached?

• Grass flowers are small and contain specialized parts. Conduct a study of various types of flowers of the grass family, including wheat, barley, oats, wild grasses, and lawn grass. Find the stamens and pistils. Use a botany book to help you identify the other additional structures in each type of flower. Summarize your findings in a comparative chart containing a sample of each flower.

• Some trees such as oak, birch, poplar, and willow have small, inconspicuous flowers arranged in catkins that appear early in the spring. Use a magnifying glass to study the structure of the flowers. What color are they? Are they complete or incomplete? How many stamens and pistils do they contain? Prepare a chart comparing these and other characteristics.

POLLEN

During self-pollination, pollen is transferred from the anther to the stigma of the same flower. When pollen is

TABLE 2. COMPARISON OF FLOWERS

Flower Parts	Name of Flower 1	Name of Flower 2	Name of Flower 3	etc.
Number of petals				
Color of petals				
Shape of petals				
Number of sepals				
Number of stamens				
Number of pistils				
Number of ovules per pistil				

transferred to the stigma of another flower, the process is called cross-pollination. Some common agents in the latter process are wind, insects, and occasionally birds.

• Self-pollination occurs in the sweet pea flower. Examine one of these flowers and carefully remove the petals. How does their arrangement lead to self-pollination and prevent cross-pollination? Where are the stamens located in relation to the stigma? If you could remove the petals without harming the rest of the flower, would cross-pollination occur? Devise a project to find the answer.

• Insects are involved in cross-pollinating the majority of flowering plants. They are attracted to the flowers by the bright colors of the petals, their fragrance, and the nectar, which serves as food. The insect feeding on the nectar comes in contact with the stamens and becomes dusted with pollen. When the insect visits another flower, the pollen rubs off on the stigma.

Observe various types of flowers. Keep a record of the color of their petals, any special arrangement of the petals, and the type of insect visitors.

• How is an orchid flower adapted for pollination? Study the anatomy of an orchid. How are the petals arranged? Do you see the "landing platform" to receive a visiting bee? Trace the passageway from there to anther and stigma. How does pollination occur?

• Conduct a project in artificial pollination. In this process, remove the stamens before they shed their pollen. Cover the remaining flower with a bag. Touch a camel's hair brush to the stamens of another flower and pick up the dustlike pollen. Remove the bag and contact the stigma lightly with the pollen on the brush. Cover the flower again with the bag. Why is this necessary? Are there advantages to artificial pollination?

• Conduct a study of pollen under the microscope. Pick up the powdery pollen (usually yellow or white) from the stamens of a flower with a small camel's hair brush and deposit a small quantity on a glass slide. Add a drop of water and apply a coverslip. Under the low power of a microscope, look for the tiny pollen grains. Switch to high power and focus on a single pollen grain. What is its shape? Is the surface smooth, or are there spines or indentations? Adding methylene blue stain may help distinguish the external features. Compare pollen grains of a number of different flowers.

• Devise a project to determine whether the pollen of wind-pollinated plants (grasses; corn; trees that have catkins, such as oak and poplar) is different from that of insect-pollinated flowers (apple, rose, and many garden flowers).

• Pollen that lands on the stigma sprouts a pollen tube (see Figure 13) that grows down the style to the ovule, where fertilization occurs. You can grow pollen tubes of an available flower (gladiolus, rose, cosmos) by placing some pollen on a slide containing a drop of a 10% solution of table sugar (sucrose). A 10% solution is prepared with 10 g of sugar dissolved in enough distilled water to make 100 mL of solution. Add a coverslip and place the slide in a moist chamber such as a covered petri dish lined with a moist paper towel. Keep the dish in a warm place. You can also use a hanging drop preparation in a depression slide. After 20 minutes, and at 10-minute intervals, examine the slide with a microscope to observe the growth of pollen tubes.

• Determine the best concentration of sugar for growing pollen tubes by using various solutions: 1%, 3%, 5%, 10%, 20%, 30%, etc.

• Compare the optimum sugar solutions for pollen tube formation in a variety of flowers. Prepare a chart of the results.

• Investigate the pollen normally contained in the air. Cover a slide with a thin film of petroleum jelly and expose it to the air in a garden for 24 hours. Using a microscope, count the number of pollen grains that settle on the slide. Record the different types. Compare the results at different locations.

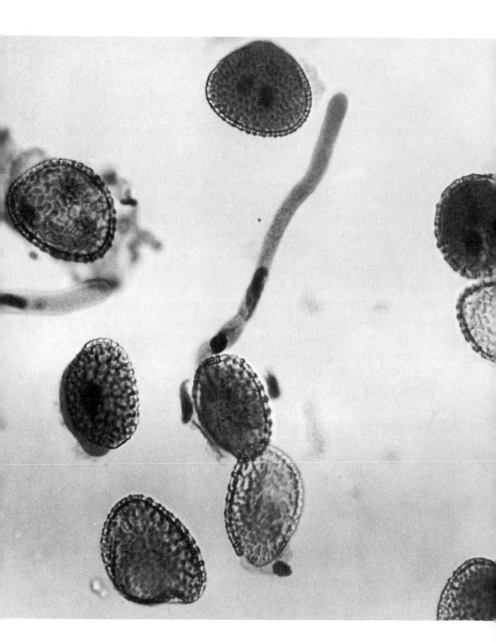

Figure 13 Pollen tubes growing from
lily pollen grains, seen under the microscope

• Look into hay fever sensitivity and the prevalence of pollen grains in the air. People who have the allergy may suffer sneezing reactions when pollens become widespread during one of the following periods: early in April, from the pollen of common wind-pollinated trees such as birch, poplar, oak, maple, and sycamore; mid-summer, from the pollinating grasses (Timothy, bluegrass, Bermuda, and Johnson grasses); from mid-August until late fall, from ragweed pollen. Expose slides coated with a thin film of petroleum jelly for 24 hours in each of these seasons. Examine the slides and make pollen counts. Compare with pollen counts at other times of the year.

FRUITS AND SEEDS

After pollination has occurred and a pollen tube has grown down through the style to the ovule, fertilization occurs. The ovule then develops into a seed, and the surrounding ovary matures into a fruit. The other parts of the flower, including the petals, sepals, stamens, stigma, and style, usually shrivel and drop off. However, in some fruits, some of these parts may still be seen. Thus the dried-up remains of the sepals may be seen at the bottom of an apple. A pea pod is also a fruit, since it is a matured ovary and contains seeds; the remains of the sepals may be seen at one end of the pod and the withered remains of the style and the stigma at the other.

• Prepare a display of different kinds of fruits to show that they are matured ovaries. Do they all have to be edible? Some fruits to try are apple, pea pod, kernel of corn (which contains one seed) or ear of corn (which is a collection of many seeds); tomato, cocklebur, winged fruit (or samara) of maple, coconut, almond, and strawberry (which is an aggregate fruit). Refer to a botany book for other examples of fruits you can include. For the display use the title "A Fruit Is a Mature Ovary of a Flower" and label each example.

• Set up an exhibit on "Vegetables That Are Fruits" containing such examples as tomatoes, cucumbers, peppers, squashes, eggplants, and bean pods. Include a short statement, with diagrams, explaining why they are technically fruits, since they developed from an ovary of a flower and contain seeds.

• When fruits ripen, their color changes and their starch is broken down by enzymes into sugars. They also produce the gas ethylene, which stimulates the ripening process. To determine the effect of ethylene on ripening, place a green banana in a small clear plastic bag containing three oranges. Seal the bag and observe whether the oranges give off enough ethylene to induce the banana to ripen faster than a control banana placed in a similar bag with three orange-size rocks.

• The ripening of a fruit is accompanied by an increase in respiration, during which oxygen is taken in. Devise a project in which the ripening of green tomatoes can be suppressed by enclosing them in a plastic bag, decreasing the amount of available oxygen. Can the same results be obtained with green bananas? Don't forget to include controls.

• A seed may be compared to a fertile chicken egg: both contain an embryo, stored food, and a covering. Conduct a study of the parts of a lima bean seed (refer to Figure 14). Soak several lima beans in water overnight. Observe the outside seed coat (the *testa*). Along the narrow end, a scar (the *hilum*) indicates the point of attachment to the ovary wall (the pod). Near it is the tiny opening (the *micropyle*) through which the pollen tube originally entered the ovule. Carefully split the bean open to reveal the two large *cotyledons,* which contain stored food. The remaining parts of the embryo consist of two tiny folded leaves *(plumules)* attached to a *hypocotyl* with its root (the *radicle*) at the other end. The lima bean is an example of the dicotyledon (dicot) group of plants, whose seeds con-

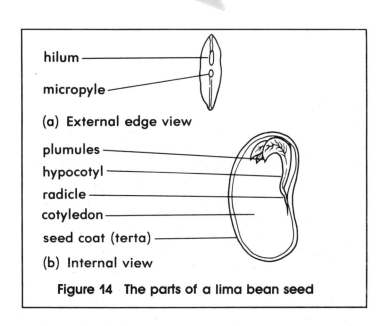

hilum ————————

micropyle ————

(a) External edge view

plumules ————————

hypocotyl ————————

radicle ————————

cotyledon ————————

seed coat (terta) ————————

(b) Internal view

Figure 14   The parts of a lima bean seed

tain two cotyledons. Prepare a display of dicot seeds (bean, pea, peanut, apple, sunflower).

• Monocotyledons (monocots) are plants whose seeds contain one cotyledon. Examples include corn, rice, wheat, rye, oat, other grasses, and lillies. Carefully remove several kernels from a fresh ear of corn. Each kernel is actually a fruit since it developed from an ovary. Examine the contents of a kernel. Refer to a botany book for details of its structure. Then set up a display of different types of monocot seeds.

• Many types of seeds store starch that will be used as food by the developing embryo when the seed germinates. To test for the presence of starch in a lima bean seed, remove the seed coat of a bean soaked overnight and apply iodine solution to the cotyledon. A blue-black color indicates the presence of starch. Make a similar study of other seeds (pea, rice, sunflower, watermelon, cucumber, pumpkin). **Safety note: Iodine is toxic. If you get any on yourself, wash it off with water.**

• Conduct a microscopic study of a seed's starch grains. Scrape the cotyledon of a lima bean with a knife and deposit a small amount of the material in a drop of water on a slide. Apply a coverslip and examine under the low power and the high power of the microscope. Stain the starch grains blue-black with iodine to make them more evident. Do this by applying a drop of iodine solution next to one side of the coverslip (not on top of it). The iodine solution will seep under the coverslip more readily if you place a piece of paper towel on the other side of the coverslip to draw the liquid through. Use this technique to make a comparative study of starch grains in other seeds. **Safety note: Iodine is toxic. If you get any on yourself, wash it off with water.**

• Many seeds and fruits have special adaptations for "leaving home," that is, spreading far from the mother plant. Otherwise, if they all germinated next to it, there would be overcrowding and competition for space, light, moisture, and minerals. Prepare a display of examples of seed and fruit dispersal by (1) wind, (2) animals, and (3) water. Collect the following:

Seeds that have special structures for being airborne: dandelion, milkweed, maple, ailanthus, elm, etc.
Fruits that are eaten by humans and other animals, which then discard or scatter their seeds: apple, pear, grape, orange, cherry, etc.
Fruits and seeds that stick to clothing or fur of passersby: cocklebur, sticktight, beggars-tick, etc.
Fruits that can float great distances on water: coconut

Write the name of the plant on a label for each example and include a brief statement about its special adaptation for seed dispersal.

5

GROWTH AND DEVELOPMENT

As every gardener and farmer knows, a new plant is born when a seed is planted and then begins to germinate. During this time, the embryo of the seed obtains its nourishment from stored food that is also part of the seed. The radicle of the embryo becomes the primary root, which grows downward to obtain moisture and to anchor the plant in the soil. The hypocotyl grows upward and develops the first leaves, which will start to carry on photosynthesis.

As the plant grows, its development is influenced by the conditions of the environment such as light, moisture, mineral supply, and temperature. Light not only supplies the energy for photosynthesis but also determines the appearance of flowers. The flowering response of plants to the length of day and night is known as *photoperiodism.*

Light also influences the direction of a plant's growth, in a response called *phototropism.* Similarly, a plant reacts to gravity: the stem and leaves grow upward, away from gravity (negative geotropism), while the roots grow downward (positive geotropism). Roots show positive *hydrotrop-*

ism by growing in the direction of water. In all of these tropisms, there is a turning or growing of the plant toward or away from the particular stimulus.

Tropisms may be explained by the action of auxin, a plant hormone. Auxin also influences growth of the stem and root. Other plant hormones produced by a plant are the *gibberellins,* which affect growth, flowering, and fruit development; and *cytokinin,* which stimulates cell division. These hormones interact with one another to produce the total growth of the plant.

SEED GERMINATION

The seed usually goes through a dormant, or resting, period after it has left the parent plant. During this time, it .... dry conditions. The chilling of seeds is known as stratification. When warmth and moisture become available, the seed germinates and forms a new plant.

• Conduct a project to determine whether seeds from McIntosh apples go through a dormancy period in which they must be chilled, or stratified, before they can germinate. Early in the fall, collect 150 well-developed seeds from recently picked McIntosh apples. To retard mold growth, soak the seeds for 1 minute in bleach solution (1 teaspoon bleach in 1 cup of water). **Safety notes: During this project, make sure you are wearing safety goggles and a lab apron. Be careful when handling bleach, since it has a strong, offensive odor. Work in a well-ventilated area, keep the bleach away from your face, and wash your hands with water when you are finished working.**

Sterilize some soil by baking it in your kitchen oven for 20 minutes at 400°F. After the soil has cooled, fill fifteen sterile petri dishes with it and moisten it with sterile water that was freshly boiled for 5 minutes and allowed to cool to room temperature. Plant ten of the treated seeds to a depth of 0.5 cm in each petri dish. Label the dishes *0* through *14* to indicate the number of weeks they are to be refrigerated. Wrap the dishes in plastic food wrap to prevent their contents from drying out.

Place the dishes labeled *1* through *14* in the refrigerator and note the temperature. Keep the dish marked *0* at room temperature. It will serve as the control. At the end of 1 week, remove the refrigerated dish labeled *1.* Unwrap it and slightly moisten the soil with freshly boiled and cooled water. Rewrap and place it alongside the control dish. Remove one of the remaining dishes every week for the next 13 weeks.

Treat the removed dishes in the following manner. Inspect them for the number of seeds that germinate. Keep daily records of all observations. In each case, how long did it take for the seeds to germinate? Did any seeds germinate before 6 weeks of stratification? Did the germination percentage increase in the seeds that were stratified for a longer period? Was the time needed for germination affected by the length of stratification?

Create a bar graph showing stratification time (on the vertical axis) and percentage of germination (on the horizontal axis). Also prepare a line graph showing the germination rate of the seeds stratified for increasing periods of time.

• Compare seed stratification in other varieties of apples, such as Golden Delicious, Red Delicious, Granny Smith, and Rome Beauty.

• It is recommended that lima beans be soaked overnight before germinating. This helps break down the seed coat. Work out a project to determine the optimum number of hours lima beans should be soaked in water before germinating.

• Grass seeds planted on a lawn require sufficient daily watering in order to sprout. Is it possible that the seed covering contains a substance that inhibits the seed from germinating until the substance has been soaked away? To find the answer, soak grass seeds in a jar of water for 24 hours. Place fifteen of the seeds in a petri dish lined with wet filter paper. Cover the dish and label it A. Keep a daily record of the seed germination.

Soak another group of seeds in the liquid remaining from the soaking of the first group of seeds. After 24 hours, place fifteen of these seeds in a similar petri dish marked B. Keep a daily record and compare the results in dishes A and B. Is there a difference in germination rates? What further steps should be taken in this investigation?

• Does light affect the rate of seed germination? Place twenty-five radish, tomato, lettuce, and grass seeds in separate closed petri dishes lined with wet filter paper. Expose them to a 100-watt bulb placed 1 meter (m) above them. Set up control dishes in the dark. Make daily observations and record the number of seeds that germinate. What do you conclude?

• Determine whether wavelength of light influences seed germination. Prepare colored cellophane envelopes of each color—red through violet—in the spectrum. Cover individual petri dishes, each containing twenty-five radish, tomato, lettuce, or grass seeds with the envelopes.

• Determine whether the age of a seed affects its ability to germinate. Place ten seeds, such as radish, from a fresh packet of seeds (look for the date stamped on it) in a petri dish lined with wet paper towel. Do the same with seeds 1 to 5 years old. Since most garden centers carry only fresh seeds, you may have to search for outdated seeds in a hardware or variety store. Keep a record of the rates of germination. What do you conclude? Some seeds have been known to germinate after a good many years. Make a study of the literature to learn more about seed longevity. One source, the 1961 **Seeds: Yearbook of Agriculture** published by the U.S. Department of Agriculture, deals with many topics relating to seeds.

• Can seeds survive after exposure to six years of radiation and vacuum in space? These are the conditions in which 12.5 million tomato seeds and 1.5 million other seeds orbited the earth in the Long Duration Exposure Facility satellite before it was brought back to earth by the space shuttle *Columbia* on January 20, 1990. Ask your teacher to write to NASA Seeds Project, Educational Affairs Division, Code XEO, NASA, Washington, DC 20546, requesting a kit containing some of these seeds and similar seeds kept on Earth as controls (see Figure 15). Plant the seeds and measure germination ability, growth rate, and length of leaves and stem. Also observe any changes in the size, color, or shape of the tomatoes produced. Do so as well with the next generation of seeds. Are there any mutations or differences from the first generation? Are there any compared with the controls? Look in future newspaper and magazine articles for reports on the experimental results involving these NASA seeds, which were distributed to schools and colleges throughout the country.

One such report in the spring of 1991 came from an elementary school principal, Robert Foerster, whose students grew the NASA seeds to maturity. He is now offering "second generation seeds" for continued study. It is likely that Mr. Foerster's school will continue to grow future generations of these tomato plants. Ask your science teacher to write for "next generation seeds," enclosing a self-addressed stamped envelope, to Robert Foerster, Principal, Burtsfield Elementary School, Next Generation Seeds, 1800 North Salisbury St., West Lafayette, IN 47906.

• The Environmental Protection Agency (EPA) has issued a preliminary report stating that the electromagnetic fields generated by common appliances and power lines may cause cancer in humans. The EPA also said that additional research is needed on this subject. Since a seed contains an embryo with living cells that multiply rapidly during germination, is there a possibility that these cells may be especially sensitive to the influence of electromagnetism? Devise a project in which you place several types of seeds on dry paper towels in petri dishes next to an electric motor (or similar source of electromagnetic in-

NASA
National Aeronautics and
Space Administration

Space Exposed Seed
Tomato Rutgers California Supreme

Park Seed Greenwood, South Carolina...Since 1868

Sealed at scientifically controlled low moisture content to
insure peak vigor in the seed until you are ready to plant.

**Figure 15   A packet of
seeds flown in space**

fluence) for a month or longer. **Work under adult super-vision.** Then add water to the paper towels and germinate these seeds. Observe whether there are any unusual results. Compare with controls. Perhaps you can try seeds of "Fast Plants" (see next section) to observe any effects on the next generation.

FAST PLANTS

A new variety of fast-growing plant has been developed by Dr. Paul H. Williams of the University of Wisconsin. The plants germinate from seeds within 12 hours of planting. Exactly 2 weeks later, when the plants are 13 cm high, yellow flowers appear. Three weeks after that, seeds are produced. Thus, the life cycle of the plant is only 35 to 40 days (see Figure 16).

The scientific name of these Fast Plants is *Brassica rapa,* and they are members of the mustard (crucifer) family. Other familiar members of the genus *Brassica* are cabbage, broccoli, cauliflower, and turnip.

Further information about *B. rapa* may be obtained from Wisconsin Fast Plants, University of Wisconsin–Madison, Department of Plant Pathology, 1630 Linden Drive, Madison, WI 53706. Seeds and growing supplies may be purchased from sources listed in the Appendix.

Because of their short life cycle, Fast Plants are ideal for laboratory and project studies. For example, try the following.

• Obtain some *B. rapa* seeds and follow the instructions for planting. Observe the growth of the plants throughout an entire life cycle. Keep a record of how much time is needed for such phases as germination; appearance of cotyledons and true leaves; elongation of the stem until flower buds appear; development of flowers; development of pods and seeds.

• Measure the daily growth of six plants for 18 days and calculate the average length for each day. Construct a growth curve of average plant height (vertical axis) relative to the number of days after planting. What is the average growth rate per day?

• Pollinate the flowers, using either a "bee-stick," as suggested in the instructional kit that comes with the Fast Plant seeds, or a small camel's hair brush. How long afterward do the pods and seeds start to develop? Extract and observe embryos at different stages of development by *carefully* cutting the pod lengthwise with a sharp knife or single-edge razor blade to expose the ovules. Also, cut the enlarging ovules open every 2 days to observe the development of the embryo. Draw a diagram showing the changing appearance of the embryo. Use a magnifying glass or a dissecting microscope (20 to 40x magnification).

• The shortness of the Fast Plant life cycle should make it possible to devise a project that reveals whether the next generation is affected by environmental influences such as exposure of the flowers to X rays (this requires **adult**

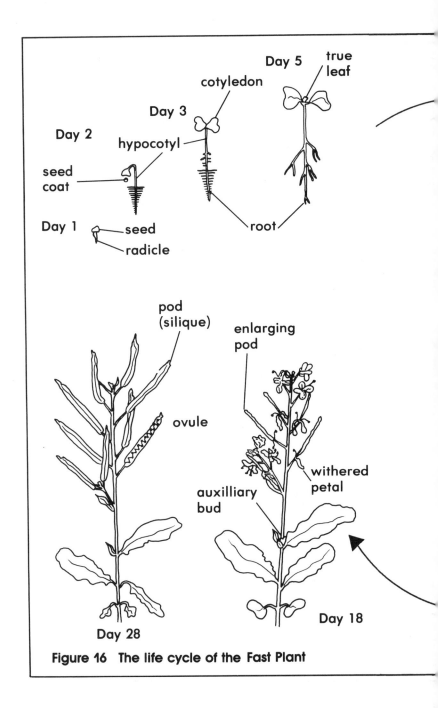

Figure 16   The life cycle of the Fast Plant

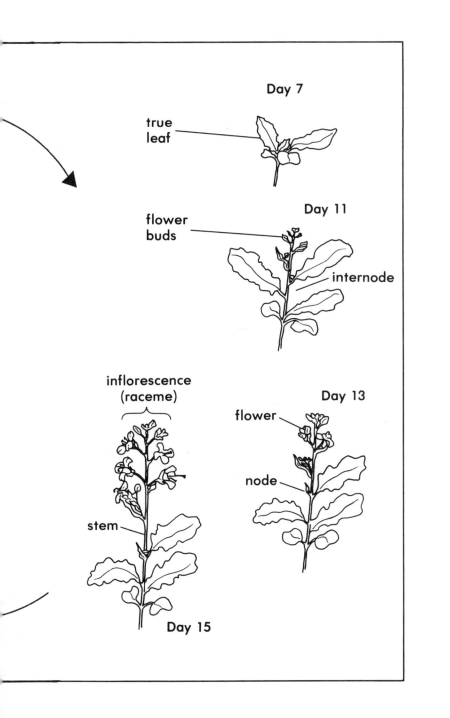

Day 7

true leaf

Day 11

flower buds

internode

inflorescence (raceme)

Day 13

flower

node

stem

Day 15

supervision), overcrowding of seedlings, liquid detergents added to the soil, or the application to the flower of a plant hormone such as gibberellin.

MINERAL REQUIREMENTS

After a seed has germinated, the young plant carries on photosynthesis and manufactures its own carbohydrates from the elements present in CO_2 and H_2O—namely, carbon, hydrogen, and oxygen. In order to grow and develop, the plant needs a number of other essential elements, especially nitrogen, phosphorus, potassium, and calcium. The elements magnesium, iron, sulfur, manganese, boron, zinc, and copper are also essential to the life of the plant.

The plant uses nitrogen, sulfur, and phosphorus to produce its proteins. Magnesium and iron are needed to produce the plant's chlorophyll. Plant scientists have discovered that a plant needs about thirty other elements—the trace elements—in minute quantities. These include chlorine, aluminum, and molybdenum.

The plant obtains all these essential and trace elements from the soil, which contains soluble mineral compounds such as nitrates, phosphates, sulfates, and potash (potassium salts). After the root hairs absorb these mineral salts, they are distributed throughout the plant by its vascular system. If the soil is deficient in the needed minerals, the plant's growth and development are adversely affected. To correct the situation, gardeners and farmers add fertilizers to the soil.

• Conduct a project to determine the effect of soil minerals on the growth of bean plants. Germinate a lima bean in each of six pots containing clean builder's sand rinsed several times in clear water to remove any impurities. The bean plants should now be growing in sand that contains no dissolved minerals.

Line a large funnel with filter paper or several layers

of cheesecloth and fill it with rich soil (either potting soil obtained at a garden center or soil you dig up (with permission, if necessary) in a wooded area. Support the funnel with a ringstand over an empty, clean, 2-L plastic soda bottle. Fill another clean soda bottle of the same size with tap water and pour it onto the soil continuously so that the excess water, which now contains dissolved soil minerals, runs out of the funnel into the bottle below it. See Figure 17.

Use this liquid to water three of the young plants. Water the other three plants with distilled water only. Keep both sets of plants under the same conditions. Record measurements of their height and other observations each day. When the plants have used up the stored food in their cotyledons, how do they compare in height and appearance? Continue with your record for at least 4 weeks. What do you observe? What do you conclude?

• How does soil from different areas (for example, an open field, a gully, a cultivated farm, and a marsh) compare in terms of the effect of their mineral content on the growth of lima bean plants germinated in pots containing washed sand?

• Compare the effect of bottled "mineral water" and distilled water on the growth of lima bean plants. (Obtain bottled "mineral water" in a grocery or supermarket.)

• Hydroponics has become a well-known method of growing plants in a water solution containing the essential elements needed for their growth. Compare the growth of plants that receive their minerals from soil with that of plants that receive their minerals from a hydroponic nutrient solution.

Germinate a bean seedling in each of two clay pots. Pot A should contain soil. Pot B should contain washed sand or vermiculite (neither of which contains dissolved minerals) and a glass wool wick that extends 5 to 8 cm out of the hole at the bottom. Place pot B in a glass battery jar containing the hydroponic nutrient (see Figure 18). You may

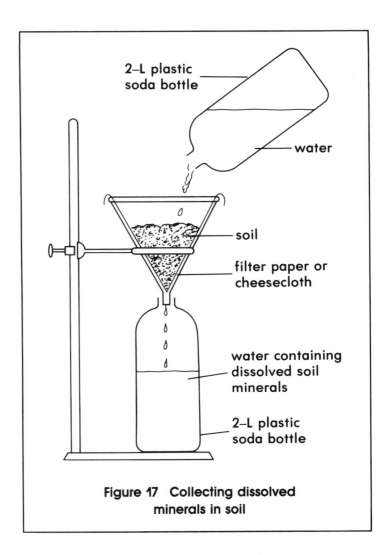

2–L plastic soda bottle

water

soil

filter paper or cheesecloth

water containing dissolved soil minerals

2–L plastic soda bottle

Figure 17 Collecting dissolved minerals in soil

use premixed hydroponic Nutri-Sol (see Appendix) or prepare your own solution from standard sources.

One of the latter solutions, Pfeffer's solution, has been in use for a long time. To prepare Pfeffer's solution, weigh each of the following salts separately, add it to a liter of distilled water, and stir. For the trace of ferric chloride, dip

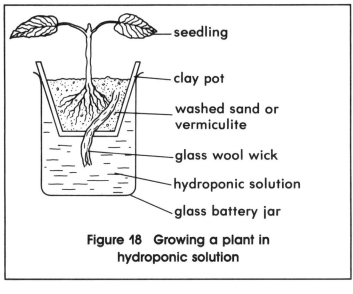

**Figure 18 Growing a plant in
hydroponic solution**

Calcium nitrate	$Ca(NO_3)_2$	0.8g
Potassium nitrate	KNO_3	0.2g
Magnesium sulfate	$MgSO \cdot 7H_2O$	0.2g
Potassium dihydrogen phosphate	KH_2PO_4	0.2g
Potassium chloride	KCl	0.2g
Ferric chloride	$FeCl_3$	trace
Distilled water	H_2O	1 L

the end of a flat toothpick into a container of ferric chloride, deposit only a small amount of it into the water, and stir. **Safety note: These salts are toxic and may be irritating to the skin, so rinse your hands with water after using each. Wear safety goggles, gloves, and a lab apron during this project.**

Cover the outside of the glass battery jar with aluminum foil to discourage the growth of algae. Place the two pots side by side. Water pot *A* regularly. Add more solution to the pot *B* setup, if necessary, so that the wick is always submerged. At weekly intervals, measure and observe the appearance of the two plants. After four weeks, compare their length and appearance. Did one of the plants grow faster? Was its appearance different? What do you conclude?

- Study the effects of a mineral deficiency. How is the plant affected by a lack of magnesium? Replace magnesium sulfate in Pfeffer's solution with sodium sulfate, Na_2SO_4. Also, what are the effects of potassium deficiency? Use $NaNO_3$ or $NaCl$ instead of KCl in the solution. **Safety note: Rinse your hands with water after using these chemicals. Wear safety goggles, gloves, and a lab apron.**

- What is the effect of excess amounts of nitrogen compounds? Double the quantity of calcium nitrate in the Pfeffer's solution formula. Also, try doubling the quantity of potassium nitrate. **Safety note: Wear safety goggles and a lab apron. Rinse your hands with water after using these chemicals.**

- Devise a project in which the roots of a plant are suspended directly in the hydroponic solution. Note: Be sure to arrange for aeration of the roots with a source of oxygen. You may want to use an aquarium pump for this purpose.

- According to a newspaper article entitled "NASA Seeks Ways of Growing Food in Space," the National Aeronautics and Space Administration is looking ahead to a time when astronauts will spend months or years in space and will grow their own food crops on a spaceship or space station or on the moon or Mars. Among the problems to be solved will be the need to provide light and minerals to plants growing in the closed system of a weightless environment.

Devise and test a project to grow a plant hydroponically under such conditions. You may want to take into account the fact that the plant could take in CO_2 exhaled by experimental animals, and that it could release O_2 into the air. You may wish to correspond with the Life Sciences Program, NASA, Washington, DC 20546, for information about ongoing projects in this challenging field.

PHOTOPERIODISM

The time of year at which a plant produces flowers is determined by the plant's exposure to the changing length of day and night during the growing seasons. This response to light and dark periods is called photoperiodism.

Plants may be classified into three main groups, according to their photoperiodism. Short-day plants, such as strawberry and chrysanthemum, flower in the spring or fall, when there are fewer than 12 to 13 hours of daylight. Long-day plants, such as apple and black-eyed Susan, flower during the early summer, when there are more than 12 hours of daylight. Day-neutrals, such as rose and tomato, do not respond to a particular length of day in producing flowers.

• Investigate the photoperiodism response of the radish plant. Plant five radish seeds in each of five separate pots. When the seeds begin to germinate, label one of the pots A and expose it to daylight, starting at 8 A.M. At 4 P.M., place the pot in a dark closet until the next morning. Continue to expose it to the light from 8 A.M. to 4 P.M. daily. Keep a record to show that pot A receives 8 hours of light.

Label another pot B and expose it to light for 10 hours, from 8 A.M. to 6 P.M. daily. Pot C receives light for 12 hours, from 8 A.M. to 8 P.M. daily. Pot D receives light for 14 hours, from 8 A.M. to 10 P.M. Where necessary, provide strong artificial illumination after daylight ends, so that the plants continue to receive their allotted amount of light. The fifth pot, E, serves as a control and is left untreated. Be careful that once a pot is placed in the dark closet, no light reaches it until 8 A.M. the next day.

Continue recording your observations daily until the plants in one of the pots develop flowers. What day length is most effective for causing radish flowers to appear? Do you need to repeat the procedure for definite proof of your conclusion?

• Determine whether the wavelength of light influences photoperiodism in radish plants. Repeat the procedures of the previous project but, this time, cover the pots with red cellophane, blue cellophane, and green cellophane envelopes.

• Find out the effects of exposing a short-day plant and a long-day plant to continuous light (24 hours daily).

• Ragweed, whose pollen causes hayfever, begins to form flower buds when the days of summer are about 14½ hours long. At the latitude of New York, this happens in July. Farther north, in Maine, it occurs in August. Early frost in that state kills the plants before the flower buds can open to release their pollen, much to the benefit of hayfever sufferers. Conduct a project to determine the relationship between latitude and ragweed growth in "hay-fever-free zones."

• The Christmas cactus can be commercially induced to produce flowers at Christmastime by limiting the amount of light it receives during the preceding 2 months. Determine which exposure to light (6, 8, 10, or 12 hours daily) is most effective in promoting flowering in the Christmas cactus.

• Can you get a Christmas cactus to produce flowers at Eastertime? When should you start your project for flowering to take place as planned?

PLANT MOVEMENT

Unlike animals, plants lack the power of locomotion. However, they do have the ability to move. They do this when they turn or grow toward or away from a stimulus. Such a response is called a tropism. The tropism is said to be positive when it is in the direction of the stimulus and negative when it is away from the stimulus. Tropisms may be responses to such stimuli as light, water, gravity and touch.

In another type of response the leaflets of the so-called sensitive plant (Mimosa pudica) fold up rapidly and the petiole droops sharply if the plant is touched. In the Venus's flytrap, two leaf blades fold over quickly to trap an insect that has touched one of three hairs on one of the blades. Other carnivorous plants, such as the sundew and the bladderwort, also trap their prey by rapid movements.

The leaves of some plants fold up at night and then open in the morning light. These so-called sleep movements seem to be controlled by an inner biological clock.

• Conduct a project to study phototropism in a geranium plant. Place the plant next to a window. After a week, observe the leaves. Have they changed their position so that they are facing the light? Turn the pot halfway around so that the leaves now face the inside of the room. Observe the position of the leaves daily. After a week, what results do you observe? Do some of the leaves turn to the left and some to the right?

• Does the very tip of the plant influence the positive phototropism of the leaves? Cover the tip with a tight cap of aluminum foil that prevents light from reaching it. Place the plant next to a window and observe it for a week. Set up a control in which the tip of a similar plant is covered with clear plastic. Is there a difference in the reactions of the plants?

• Do different wavelengths of light affect phototropism? Construct a large envelope of blue cellophane and fit it over a geranium plant. Prepare similar envelopes of red cellophane, green cellophane, and colorless cellophane for other geranium plants. Place all the setups next to a window and observe the results for a week. What do you conclude? What was the purpose of using colorless cellophane?

• How do roots react to a source of moisture? Germinate six lima bean seedlings on moist paper towel. When the roots are 2 to 5 cm long, place the seedlings at 5-cm intervals, with the roots pointing downward, against the glass of a dry aquarium containing dry vermiculite or sand. Insert a large sponge against the glass at the far end of the aquarium. See Figure 19. Water the sponge liberally every

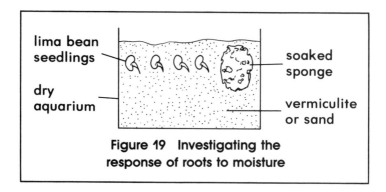

Figure 19 Investigating the response of roots to moisture

lima bean seedlings

dry aquarium

soaked sponge

vermiculite or sand

day. It will serve as the only source of moisture available to the roots. Observe the roots daily for a week and keep a record of their growth. Do you see evidence of positive hydrotropism? Account for any difference in the direction of root growth.

• Investigate the effect of gravity on the growth of seedlings. Germinate six lima bean or radish seeds on wet filter paper in a petri dish. When the seedlings have developed, place the root ends in test tubes lined on half the inside with wet paper towels. Gently install absorbent cotton around the opening of the test tubes to hold the plants in place, with the stems protruding from the test tubes. See Figure 20.

Support one of the test tubes right side up on a ringstand. Place another upside down, a third in a horizontal position, a fourth diagonally with the stem facing up, and a fifth diagonally with the stem facing down. Observe the growth of the roots and the stems. Keep a daily record and draw a sketch to show their appearance. After a week, what do you conclude about the geotropic response of roots and stems?

• How does altered gravitational influence such as centrifugal motion affect the response of seedlings? At-

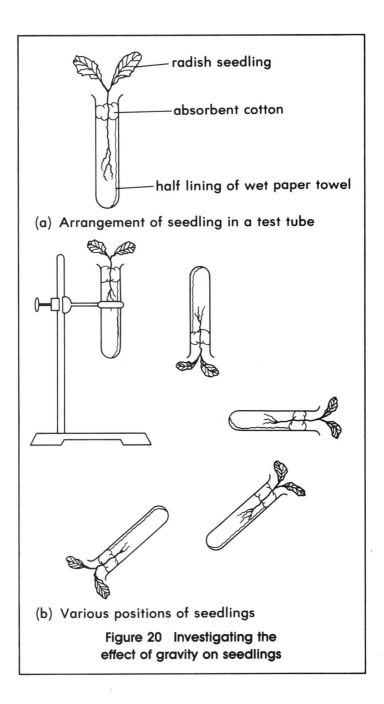

radish seedling

absorbent cotton

half lining of wet paper towel

(a) Arrangement of seedling in a test tube

(b) Various positions of seedlings

Figure 20 Investigating the effect of gravity on seedlings

tach a test tube containing a seedling to a rotating device that is constantly turning (for example, a clock or motor). After a week, observe the direction of root and stem growth. Investigate the effect of speeding up the rotation rate; also investigate the effect of reversing the direction of the rotation.

• NASA welcomes suggestions from students for experiments that can be conducted in the weightless conditions of space on the proposed space station. Consider submitting a proposal on the geotropic response of seedlings under conditions of zero gravity. Describe the details, with a diagram, showing your suggested setup. Write to Space Science Student Involvement Program, NASA, Washington, DC 20546.

• Does a morning glory vine grow in a clockwise or counter-clockwise direction during a thigmotropism response? How many plants should you grow to seek an answer to this question? Why?

• What is the effect of a mechanical action, such as rubbing the leaves of a plant, on its growth? (Such an effect is called thigmomorphogenesis.) Germinate six lima bean seeds in separate containers. When the first leaves have developed, start the rubbing activity as follows. Rub one of the primary leaves twice—once up and once down—between the thumb and forefinger, with moderate pressure. Label this plant 2 (the 2 stands for *two rubbings*). Treat each of four other plants similarly, but vary the number of rubbings to five, ten, twenty, and thirty rubs each; label the plants accordingly. The last plant is the control and is labeled 0, to show that there has been no rubbing. Keep the plants next to each other, and measure their height with a centimeter ruler daily for 3 weeks. Rub the leaves at the same time daily for the 3-week period. Record your results in a table. What do you observe? At the end of the 3-week period, also measure the thickness of the stems at the level of the primary leaves. Is there a difference? What do you conclude?

• Investigate the response of a sensitive plant *(Mimosa pudica)* to touch (see Figure 21). Grow the plant from seed or order one from a plant nursery. Try varying amounts of stimulation on the tip of a leaf by gently touching it with a camel's hair brush, tapping it with a pencil, or sharply striking it with the handle of a spoon. Allow the leaf to "recover" before proceeding with the next stimulus. Describe the response of the leaflets and the petiole in each case. Use a watch with a second hand to measure the length of time needed by the leaf to return to its normal position after each stimulus. What do you conclude?

• Which is the most sensitive part of the *Mimosa* leaf: the tip, the middle, or the base? Observe the reactions in each case, measure the time and record your results.

• Study the insectivorous plant, Venus' flytrap. Touch the point of a pencil to various parts of the leaf. Under what circumstances will the trap close? Will it respond to stimuli other than touch?

• Observe sleep movements in a lima bean seedling. Germinate a lima bean in a flower pot and keep it near a window. When the primary leaves develop, keep a record of their position at 3:00 P.M., 9:00 P.M., 11 P.M., 2:00 A.M., 12 noon, and other times. Do the leaves droop at any time? Using the same time intervals, observe another plant that is kept in a closet for 24 hours. Do its leaves also show sleep movements? Explain your results. Take photographs of the plants at the different time intervals to show the position of the leaves.

• Can you measure the amount of leaf movement? Cut a small pointer about 2 to 3 cm long from a soda straw and use a drop of white glue to attach it to the end of the primary leaves of a young lima bean seedling. Use a ringstand to hold a centimeter ruler in place next to this pointer, as shown in Figure 22. Keep a record of the reading. Make readings every three hours of the day and night (or more frequently, if possible). Construct a graph to show the extent of leaf movement in a 24-hour day.

Figure 21   The undisturbed
sensitive plant (top) responds
to touch by curling its leaves.

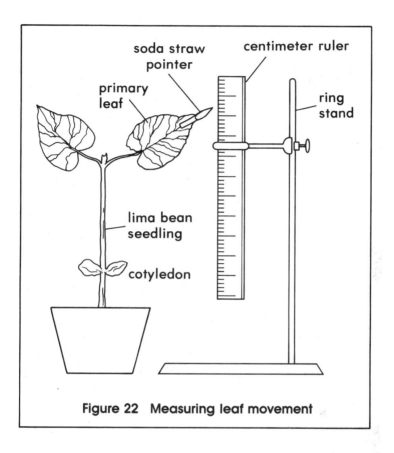

Figure 22   Measuring leaf movement

• Make a study of sleep movements in other members of the legume family (for example, clover, sensitive plant, honey locust tree). Keep a record of the time of day when these movements occur. Are they the same on sunny, rainy, and cloudy days?

• Make a study of flowers that open and close at different times of the day (for example, morning glory, evening primrose, and four-o'clock). Prepare a chart.

HORMONES

In addition to external factors that influence a plant's growth (light, water, minerals, and so on), there are also hormones formed by the plant itself that regulate its development. The best known of these hormones are auxins and gibberellins; others include cytokinins and ethylene.

Auxins, produced in the growing tip of the stem and leaves, promote growth by stimulating cell elongation. They also influence plants in other ways: they promote the growth of the terminal bud and inhibit growth in lateral buds; they are active in the phototropism response of plants; they are used to control weeds by abnormally speeding up their rate of growth, causing them to die; they induce root formation in cuttings; they prevent apples from dropping from trees prematurely; when sprayed on tomato flowers, they result in seedless tomatoes.

Gibberellins also promote plant growth, causing an increase in height. In addition, they cause such other effects as: making dwarf plants grow to normal size; causing seeds that are soaked in them to germinate faster; influencing some biennial plants (for example, foxglove, carrot, and cabbage) to flower in the first season; changing the photoperiod of long-day plants (for example, radish and lettuce) so that they bloom under short-day periods; and making some plants (for example, geranium and petunia) bloom faster and produce larger flowers.

Cytokinins, which were originally discovered in coconut milk, have also been found in seeds, fruit, and roots of plants. They stimulate cell division. They also have been found to act in opposition to auxins by promoting the growth of lateral buds, not terminal buds. When used with auxins, they can cause small sections of plant tissue growing in tissue culture to differentiate into roots, stems, and leaves.

• In 1926, the botanist F.W. Went isolated the first plant hormone from the tips of oat coleoptiles and named it

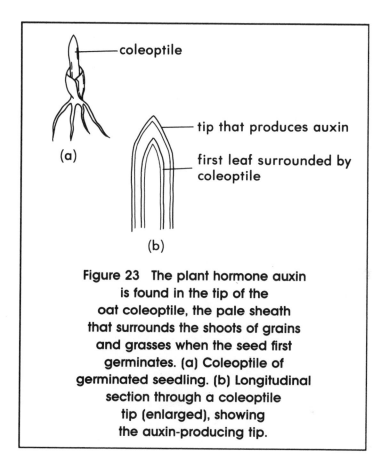

coleoptile

tip that produces auxin

first leaf surrounded by coleoptile

(a)

(b)

Figure 23 The plant hormone auxin is found in the tip of the oat coleoptile, the pale sheath that surrounds the shoots of grains and grasses when the seed first germinates. (a) Coleoptile of germinated seedling. (b) Longitudinal section through a coleoptile tip (enlarged), showing the auxin-producing tip.

auxin. See Figure 23. The coleoptile is the pale sheath that surrounds the shoot of grains and other grasses when the seed first germinates. Follow in Went's footsteps and investigate how auxin affects the growth of oat seedlings.

How does auxin from the tip of a coleoptile affect growth? Plant twenty oat seeds in individual containers of moist soil and keep them in the dark. When the seeds germinate, use a sharp single-edge razor to *carefully* cut a piece about 2 to 3 mm long from the tips of two coleoptiles about 2 cm high. Replace the tip on one coleoptile; leave the stump of the other coleoptile uncovered. Continue to keep both seedlings in the dark. After 6 hours, compare the length of both coleoptiles. Explain your result.

• Does auxin absorbed in an agar block affect growth? Carefully cut the tips off five coleoptiles and place four of them on a freshly prepared thin layer of agar allowed to cool and harden (Figure 24a). Leave the tips there for 1, 2, 3, and 4 hours, respectively. Then cut out a small block of the agar directly beneath each coleoptile tip. You can now discard the tips. Place the agar blocks on the coleoptile stumps (Figure 24b). As a control, place an agar block that did not have a tip resting on it on the fifth coleoptile stump. Keep all the seedlings in the dark. After 6 hours, measure the length of each coleoptile. What effect did the treated agar blocks have on them? Explain any differences in their length.

• How does auxin affect one side of a coleoptile? Repeat the previous procedure. This time, however, cover only the right half of the tops of the stumps with a treated agar block (Figure 24c). Use an untreated agar block as a control. Keep the seedlings in the dark. After 6 hours, observe the appearance of the coleoptile stumps. How were they affected by the one-sided placement of the agar blocks? Explain the results. Does this help you explain the positive phototropism of a stem that occurs in response to a source of light coming from one side?

• Conduct similar projects with corn seedlings, which have larger coleoptiles than those of oats. Would you expect the results to be the same?

• After Dr. Went's discovery of auxin, its chemical composition was found to be that of indoleacetic acid (IAA). Other, similar chemical compounds not produced by plants have also been found to have growth-producing properties, for example, napthaleneacetic acid, indolebutyric acid, and 2,4-D (dichlorophenoxyacetic acid). All

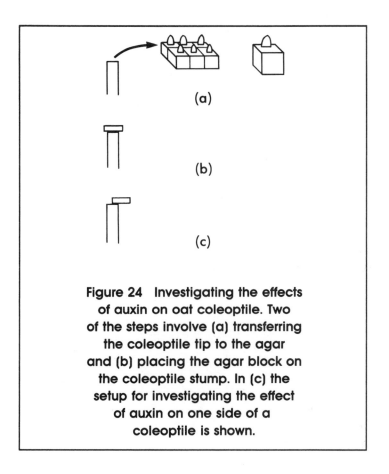

Figure 24 Investigating the effects of auxin on oat coleoptile. Two of the steps involve (a) transferring the coleoptile tip to the agar and (b) placing the agar block on the coleoptile stump. In (c) the setup for investigating the effect of auxin on one side of a coleoptile is shown.

of these are sold under various trade names at garden supply centers. **Safety notes: Work under supervision. Wear safety goggles, gloves, and a lab apron. If you spill any of these chemicals on yourself, wash it off with water.**

Conduct a project to initiate the development of a tomato ovary without pollination taking place. Spray a newly opened tomato flower with an auxin product such as To-matotone or Fruitone. (Why should you first remove the stamens carefully with tweezers?) Will you cover the flower with a bag after spraying? Why? Be sure to set up a control by treating a similar flower in the same way, using water instead of the auxin compound. Why is this necessary? Observe the development of both flowers. Do you expect the experimental flower to produce seeds? Why? What happens to the control flower?

• Investigate the effect of auxin on root formation in cuttings. Obtain an auxin compound such as Rootone and follow the directions to induce root formation in various types of cuttings of house plants, such as geranium and coleus, and woody plants, such as lilac and forsythia. Keep a record of the number of days required for roots to appear. Compare with controls.

• What effect does auxin have on the growth of a lima bean plant? Germinate six lima bean seeds in individual containers. When the plants have developed their first leaves, apply auxin (for example, Hormodin) powder or liquid to three small wads of absorbent cotton. **Safety notes: Wear safety goggles. Avoid inhaling the powder. Wash your hands with water after any contact with the chemical.**

Gently but firmly wrap the cotton around the stem of each of three plants, halfway between the leaves and the cotyledons. Keep the wads in place with small adhesive bandages. See Figure 25. Treat the other three plants similarly, placing water or talcum power on the absorbent cotton wads instead of auxin. These are the controls. Keep the plants next to each other on a windowsill. After one week, use a millimeter ruler to measure the length of each stem. Calculate the average length for each group. Is there a difference in length? Are there any other observable differences?

• How do gibberellins affect the growth of dwarf pea plants? You may have learned about Gregor Mendel's classic experiments in which he studied the heredity of tall pea plants that grew to a height of about 2 m and dwarf pea plants that grew only to about 0.5 m. Obtain a gib-

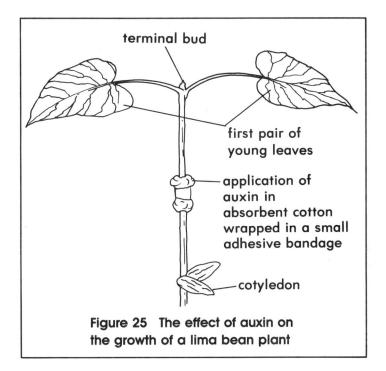

terminal bud

first pair of
young leaves

application of
auxin in
absorbent cotton
wrapped in a small
adhesive bandage

cotyledon

**Figure 25 The effect of auxin on
the growth of a lima bean plant**

berellin preparation, such as Gibrel or Wonder-brel, at a
garden center and study its effect on the growth of dwarf
pea plants. (Dwarf pea seeds are obtainable from a biological supply company. See Appendix.) **Safety note: Wear
safety goggles. Wash your hands with water after handling gibberellin products.**

Divide the seeds into two groups, A and B. In group A,
soak three seeds in gibberellin solution for 6 hours. Soak
three other seeds for 12 hours, and three more seeds for
24 hours. Include similar control seeds soaked in water.
Plant the seeds in pots and observe their growth for 1 month.
Measure the length of the experimental and control plants
daily. In group B, plant in separate pots six seeds soaked
in water overnight. When the young seedlings appear, spray

three of them lightly with an aerosol form of gibberellin. Spray the other three lightly with water. Continue to spray both sets of plants lightly every day for a month. Measure their length daily. What conclusions do you draw?

Since Mendel showed that dwarfism in peas is an inherited trait, one can speculate that these plants are missing the gene to form gibberellin.

• Investigate the effect of gibberellin on the germination and development rate of seeds. Soak seeds (for example, radish, lima bean, cucumber, tomato) in gibberellin solution overnight. Compare their germination rate with that of control seeds soaked in water.

• How do gibberellins influence size and flowering in geranium plants? Follow the directions on an aerosol form of gibberellin (for example, Wonder-brel) and spray a geranium. Spray a control plant of equal size with water. Place the two plants next to each other on a windowsill. Keep a weekly record of the size and appearance of both plants. Make a note of any differences in flowering. **Safety note: Wash your hands with water after working with gibberellin products.**

• Cytokinins (first known as kinetin) were discovered when coconut milk was found to stimulate growth and differentiation in isolated tissues of plant cells growing on a sterile culture medium in test tubes. This tissue-culture technique would be difficult for most students because it requires laboratory training in aseptic methods—that is, methods that involve keeping all materials free of bacteria and molds. Nevertheless, knowing that cytokinins stimulate cell division, see whether you can devise a project in which you apply coconut milk to parts of plants that have actively dividing cells, such as germinating seeds, root tips, and the tips of stems.

To prepare coconut milk, follow these steps. Use a cork borer to remove one of the three "eyes" at the end of a coconut, which is composed of relatively soft tissue. Puncture one of the other "eyes" with an electric drill or a hammer and large nail. **Be careful in handling these tools.** The coconut liquid will now flow out freely. Filter it through several layers of cheesecloth. Boil the filtered liquid for 10 minutes to precipitate the protein. After the liquid has cooled to room temperature, pass it through filter paper. The final coconut milk extract can be frozen for use at a later date. Thawing and refreezing do not diminish the properties of the cytokinins present in the liquid.

• If possible, learn the techniques involved in tissue culture. (See the end of the next chapter.) If you decide to use coconut milk in a tissue culture project, you can use 100–150 mL of the extract in making up 1 L of the tissue culture nutrient medium.

6

HEREDITY

A planted acorn develops into an oak tree, not a maple. A tomato seed produces a tomato plant when it germinates, not a rosebush. Each type of plant has genes that it received from its parent plants and that determine its development.

Long before we knew about genes, an Austrian monk named Gregor Mendel (1822–1884) experimented with pea plants in his monastery garden and made important discoveries about traits that are dominant and recessive and processes such as segregation and independent assortment. Mendel was successful in his work largely because he started out by following the inheritance of one trait at a time, tracing first the plants' height (tall is dominant, dwarf is recessive), then the color of the seeds (yellow is dominant, green is recessive), then the texture of the surface of the seeds (smooth is dominant, wrinkled is recessive), and so on.

He carefully cross-pollinated plants showing these contrasting characteristics without letting stray pollen interfere with his results. He also patiently kept accurate records of large numbers of plants and seeds. Thus, he was able to make conclusions on the basis of the consistent numerical ratios he calculated.

Unfortunately, his 1865 paper "Experiments in Plant Hybridization" did not receive recognition until 1900, when it was rediscovered and served as the basis of the new science of genetics. His discoveries were found to apply to all kinds of other plants and to animals as well, including human beings. You may want to read a biology textbook to find out more about Mendel's contributions and method of work.

In some types of inheritance, Mendel's idea of dominance does not apply. Thus, there is a blending of color in the snapdragon flower. When red and white snapdragons are cross-pollinated, all the offspring have pink flowers. Then, when these pink flowers are cross-pollinated, the next generation shows the three colors in a 1:2:1 ratio, or 25 percent red, 50 percent pink, and 25 percent white.

Relatively recent discoveries have revealed that genes are segments of the DNA molecule. DNA—deoxyribonucleic acid—is a double-helical (that is, two-spiralled) molecule present in the chromosomes of a cell. It carries the genetic code, or heredity pattern, of the individual. DNA is present in plants as well as in animals. When the chromosomes divide during mitosis, or cell division, the DNA replicates itself and passes equally into the new cells.

As a rule, DNA replicates itself exactly and passes the same genetic code on to the new cells. At times, however, a change may occur in the molecular structure of DNA that will alter the characteristics inherited. Such a change is called a gene mutation. Inherited changes may also be caused by chromosome mutations. Mutations may arise from an imperfection in replication, or may be due to environmental influences such as chemicals, X rays, radioactivity, or cosmic rays. Since they tend to upset the genetic makeup of an organism, mutations are generally harmful. However, in a number of cases (for example, the seedless orange), they are useful.

In order for genes to exert their effect completely, the proper environmental conditions must be present. A plant that has genes for the formation of chlorophyll will not turn green if it is germinated in the dark. Corn plants deprived of essential minerals in the soil will yield a poor crop. In other words, a plant is a product of both its heredity and its environment.

When a plant reproduces by means of seeds, the resulting offspring show a variety of characteristics, depending on the different genes combined during fertilization. However, when a plant reproduces directly from a stem, leaf, or root, its offspring are identical to it because they have the same genetic makeup; no new genes are involved. Such an organism, which has the same set of genes as its parent plants, is called a *clone*.

• Find out how the laws of probability apply to segregation. Obtain one package each of dried yellow split peas and green split peas at a grocery store. Count 50 of each and place them in a wide-mouthed jar labeled A. Mix them up thoroughly. Do the same for another jar labeled B. There are now 100 mixed split peas in each jar. Assume that jar A represents the stamen of a flower and that each split pea is the sperm nucleus or male gamete in the pollen containing the gene for that color. Similarly, jar B represents the ovule, and each split pea represents the egg nucleus of female gamete containing the gene for that color.

With your right hand, reach into jar A and withdraw one split pea. Avoid looking into the jar—you want the selection to be random. Do the same with your left hand and jar B. Place the new pair of peas, representing the fertilized egg, in one of three bottles that you have previously labeled Yellow-Yellow, Yellow-Green, and Green-Green. (For example, if you have selected one yellow and one green pea, place the two peas into the *Yellow-Green* bottle.) Continue this procedure until you have removed all the split peas from the jars. Count the number of peas in each bottle, divide that number by 2 to obtain the number of pairs, and record the result in the following order:

Yellow-Yellow ___; Yellow-Green ___; Green-Green ___.

Did you expect to find a ratio of 1:2:1? Why? How close to that ratio do your actual results lie? Explain any differences. Repeat the experiment with another set of yellow and green split peas. What are the counts this time? Now add the two experimental results together. How different is the result from those of each experiment taken individually? Repeat the experiment three more times so that you end up having studied a grand total of 500 split peas. Record the results each time, and add them to your previous totals. What does the final outcome show? What is your conclusion about the number of random trials and the predicted ratios?

When Mendel was doing his experiments on pea plants, one of the characteristics he studied was the color of the seeds. He found that yellow is dominant and green is recessive. His second-generation (F_2) counts were 6,022 yellow and 2,001 green, a ratio of 3.01:1. This was one of the results that led him to formulate the Principle of Segregation. (When hybrids are crossed, the genes separate into different gametes and then recombine to produce dominant and recessive offspring in a ratio of 3:1). How do your results compare? Explain any differences.

• Follow in Mendel's footsteps and grow dwarf and tall pea plants. You can plant them outdoors, or indoors using either large flower pots or the bottom halves of half-gallon milk containers, which are usually suitable for a 2½-month growing period.

Start by soaking the seeds for tall plants overnight. Use only seeds that show signs of germinating after the soaking and plant them about 2.5 cm deep. Keep the soil moist by regular watering, but do not soak it. Since tall pea plants usually produce flowers later than dwarf plants do, their seeds should be planted 15 days ahead of those of the dwarf strain; this will allow flowers of both varieties to be ready for cross-pollination at about the same time, 75 to 80 days later.

Record measurements of the heights of both types. When the flower buds form, they are ready for the first step in cross-pollination. Gently open a bud of a dwarf plant and snip out the unripe stamens. Cover it with a small plastic or paper bag to prevent stray pollen from reaching it. When the blossoms mature, cross-pollinate by transferring pollen with a small camel's hair brush from the ripe stamens of a tall plant to the stigma of the prepared short-plant blossom. Cover the prepared flower again. Label the plants for your record. Also transfer pollen from a short plant to the stigma of a tall plant. As a control, and as a check on the purity of the varieties, allow other flowers to self-pollinate; cover the buds with a paper bag when they appear.

Allow the pods to remain on the plants until they have thoroughly dried and have begun to split open. Then collect the seeds, which represent the F_1 hybrids. When you plant these seeds, how tall will the plants be? Cross-pollinate their flowers and collect the resulting F_2 seeds. Plant them and keep a weekly record of the height of the plants. Calculate the ratio. Compare your results with Mendel's. He tabulated 787 tall: 277 dwarf, for a ratio of 2.84:1.

• Conduct a similar project to investigate the inheritance of smooth and wrinkled peas. When Mendel studied this characteristic, he tabulated 5,474 smooth seeds and 1,850 wrinkled seeds in the F_2 generation, for a ratio of 2.96:1. How do your results compare? Account for any differences.

• Compare the microscopic differences inherited in the starch grains of smooth and wrinkled peas. Soak a half-dozen of both types of seeds overnight. *Carefully* use a sharp single-edged razor blade to slice a soaked smooth pea in half and scrape a tiny amount from the cut surface into a drop of water on a microscope slide. Mix thoroughly with a toothpick and apply a coverslip. Prepare a similar slide for a soaked wrinkled pea. Examine the slides under the low and high power of the microscope. Do the starch grains appear smooth or uneven? Are all the starch grains alike on each slide? What is the explanation for your answer? Draw a diagram of the starch grains. How does a drop of iodine solution on the slide affect the appearance of the starch grains? **Safety note: Iodine is toxic. If you spill any on yourself, wash it off with water.**

• Cross tall pea plants that produce smooth seeds with dwarf pea plants that produce wrinkled seeds. Study the appearance of the F_2 generation. Why would you expect your results to illustrate Mendel's Principle of Independent Assortment (traits are inherited independently of each other)? Compare your ratio with his. Account for any differences.

• Investigate codominance in the snapdragon by planting seeds for red and for white flowers. When the flowers develop, cross-pollinate them in the standard way, following the suggested steps to prevent self-pollination or pollination by stray pollen. Collect the seeds of the F_1 generation and plant them. What color(s) do you obtain? Now cross-pollinate the F_1 flowers (or self-pollinate them by covering them with paper bags before the buds open). Plant the seeds of the F_2 generation. What colors show up? Tabulate the numbers of each color. Is this what you expected? Why?

• What are the results if you hybridize morning glory plants? Obtain seeds for a blue variety and for those of another color—for example, white. Soak them overnight and plant them in separate containers, such as flower pots or the bottom parts of half-gallon milk containers. Insert a vertical stake in each for the plants to wind about. As the plants develop, pinch off the top buds of both the main stem and the branches to encourage bushy growth, which makes them easier to handle. When a flower bud appears to be ready to open, *carefully* slit it down the side with a single-edge razor blade and remove the immature stamens with tweezers. Cover the bud with a small plastic bag to keep unwanted pollen away.

When the flower opens, use a camel's hair brush to transfer pollen to its stigma from a flower of the other color. Record the colors of the flowers involved and the date. When the seed pod forms, allow it to develop until it dries completely. Then collect the hybrid seeds and plant them. Record the colors of the flowers that develop and compare with the colors of the parent flowers. Allow these hybrid flowers to self-pollinate by covering them with plastic bags to prevent accidental cross-pollination. Plant the seeds for the F_2 generation. Record the colors produced. How many of each are there? Explain the results. Devise other crosses. Can you predict the results?

• Study albinism in corn. This is a recessive trait that results in the ultimate death of the young seedling because of an inability to produce chlorophyll. Obtain hybrid corn seeds that contain the dominant gene for the normal green trait and the recessive gene for albinism. After you plant the seeds in twelve individual large containers, they will germinate within 2 weeks. Predict how many albino plants will appear. How many actually appear? How long do they remain alive?

• Attempt to devise techniques for growing albino corn to maturity.

• Living things differ from one another because of the effects of heredity and environment. Investigate the accuracy of the expression "as alike as two peas in a pod." Open a pea pod and observe the number and the attachment of the peas inside. Remove the peas and place them next to each other. Are they all identical in size and shape? Open at least six more pods and count the number of peas in each. Compare the peas with one another. Arrange all the peas next to each other according to size, with the smallest at the left and the largest at the right. How do you account for the differences, if any, in size?

Prepare a display board with the title "as alike as two peas in a pod(?)" and paste on it pods showing the arrangement of the peas, and all the peas according to size.

• Investigate variation in tree leaves. Although the tree developed from one seed and all its leaves inherited the same genes, are these leaves identical in size, shape, and appearance? Collect fifteen leaves from a tree. (If the tree is on private property, be sure to ask for permission.) Press them for 2 weeks and prepare a display demonstrating any variation in their appearance. Account for any differences.

• Investigate variation in lima beans. Use a millimeter ruler to measure the lengths of 300 beans. As you measure each bean, deposit it in a test tube labeled for its particular length. Arrange the test tubes next to each other in a test tube rack, with the smallest beans on the left, and the longest on the right. Count the number of beans in each test tube and record the results in a table. Prepare a graph to show the distribution of the beans. How does the graph compare with the distribution of the beans in the test tubes?

• Can selective breeding produce lima beans that are either small or large? Plant the smallest and largest beans of the preceding project. When the flowers begin to appear, self-pollinate them by covering them with plastic bags. Allow the pods to ripen fully and dry up before you collect the lima beans. Measure the lengths of the beans. Compare with the first group of beans. Repeat the procedure for as many generations as possible. Prepare graphs for each generation to show the extent of the variations in each case. Compare the results with what you found when you examined the original set of unselected beans. Summarize your findings on the effects of selective breeding.

• How does the environment influence the action of genes? Soak ten lima beans in water overnight. Plant them in individual containers. Place five of the containers (group A) in a closet where no light can reach them. Leave the others (group B) on a windowsill where they are exposed to daylight. Water both sets of plants when the soil appears dry. As the beans in group *B* germinate, what is the color of their leaves? Compare with the leaves in group *A*. Account for the difference. After 2 to 3 weeks, transfer group *A* to the light. Do the genes for chlorophyll formation now exert their effect?

• How does overcrowding affect the action of genes? Soak forty-two sunflower seeds in water overnight. Obtain three empty half-gallon milk containers. Rinse them and cut off their tops. Fill each with good soil. Plant two seeds in the first container, eight seeds in the second container, and thirty-two seeds in the third. When the seeds have sprouted, thin them to one, four, and sixteen healthy plants, respectively. Try to distribute the plants evenly in their containers. Water the plants when the topsoil becomes dry, but do not soak the soil. Place the containers next to each other so they are exposed to equal amounts of light.

When the single plant in the first container has grown to a height of 45 cm, cut all the plants at soil level. Record the following data for each plant: height; diameter of stem immediately above cotyledons; number of leaves; length and width of the largest leaf; weight. Compare the average for the plants in each container. Prepare and interpret bar graphs of the results.

CLONES—DESCENDANTS WITH IDENTICAL GENES

Not all plants reproduce only by means of flowers that form seeds. Some can reproduce from leaves, stems, or roots. This method of reproduction is called *vegetative propagation.* Since only one parent plant is involved, the new offspring are different in one important respect from those produced by flowers: They contain the same genes as their parent and so are exactly like the original plant. As you read earlier, such plants are known as clones.

In recent years, plants have also been made to reproduce by tissue culture techniques, in which a very small part of a plant is grown in a flask that contains a supply of nutrients. The plant that develops is also a clone. Since it contains the same genes, it is identical to the parent plant.

• How can new plants be produced from a single leaf? Remove a leaf from a *Bryophyllum* plant. Lay it down on moist soil in a flower pot. Observe it daily and water the soil lightly so that it does not dry out. How many new plants begin to form on the leaf? From what part of the leaf do they develop? As the little plants develop roots, cut the plants from the original leaf and plant them in small pots.

• Will a *Bryophyllum* leaf produce new plants if it is merely placed in a moist chamber, such as a covered shallow jar that does not contain soil? Spray the leaf lightly with water from time to time if it appears to dry out. Keep a record of developments.

• Propagate leaf cuttings of other plants, such as *Kalanchoe, Sansevieria, Pepperomia,* begonia, and African violet.

• Can plants be propagated from stem cuttings? Select several plants such as begonia, coleus, geranium, and willow. *Carefully* cut the stem under water at a slant with a clean, sharp knife just below a node, the spot where a leaf arises. The cutting should be about 12 to 15 cm long. Remove the lower leaves, preserving several leaves near the tip. Place the stem of each cutting in a separate jar of water. Observe weekly and keep a record of root formation. Then plant the cuttings in flower pots of moist soil. How do the new plants compare with the original?

• How does auxin improve root formation in cuttings? Cut a 12- to 15-cm stem slantwise just below a node, from a plant such as coleus or geranium. Remove the lower leaves. Dip the cut end of the stem into auxin (for example, Hormodin or Rootone). Tap the stem to remove excess powder. With a pencil, make a planting hole in moist sand in a flower pot. **Safety note: Wash carefully if you spill any of these products on yourself.**

Then carefully insert the stem to a depth of 3 to 4 cm without rubbing off the hormone. Pat the sand into place

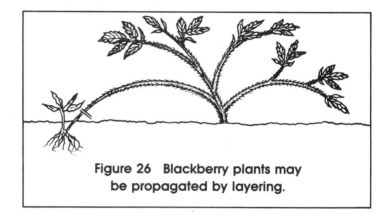

Figure 26   Blackberry plants may be propagated by layering.

around the stem. Keep the sand moist but not soaked. Prepare a similar stem cutting as a control, but treat it with talcum powder. Cover the cuttings with plastic bags, and keep them out of direct sunlight. After 2 to 3 weeks, gently tug each cutting. If rooting has occurred, the plant will resist being pulled out. How effective was the auxin treatment?

• Will the stem cutting of a woody plant form roots? Repeat the previous procedure, using such plants as rose, hydrangea, weigela, and magnolia.

• Can new plants be propagated by layering? In this procedure, select the young lower stem of a plant (for example, blackberry) and make a slight cut in the bark. Wear heavy gloves to protect against thorns. Dust the wound with rooting hormone, then bury that part of the stem under 5 to 8 cm of soil, as shown in Figure 26. Hold the stem in place with a rock on top of the soil. Roots may take several months to develop. One way to check for roots is to feel for them in the soil. After roots have formed, cut the layered stem from the parent plant and treat it like a stem cutting. Place the stem in a pot of soil, and keep it moist and partially shaded until it becomes well established.

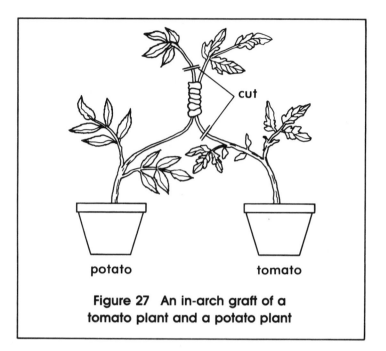

cut

potato   tomato

**Figure 27   An in-arch graft of a
tomato plant and a potato plant**

• In grafting, a bud or a stem (the scion) is cut from
one plant and attached to another plant (the stock), which
furnishes it with water and minerals as well as support.
However, the scion has its own genes and will produce
flowers, fruits, and seeds of its own kind.

Conduct a project in which you attach a tomato plant
to a potato plant by an "in-arch" graft. Start with a tomato
plant and a potato plant in separate pots. When they are
about 25 cm tall, carefully slice off enough tissue from the
side of each stem to expose a few vascular bundles. Do
this about one-third to one-half of the way down the stem
from the top. Gently but firmly tie the stems together with
raffia or similar material so that the exposed vascular bundles are in close contact. Cover the area of attachment
with grafting wax or paraffin that has been **carefully
heated.** See Figure 27.

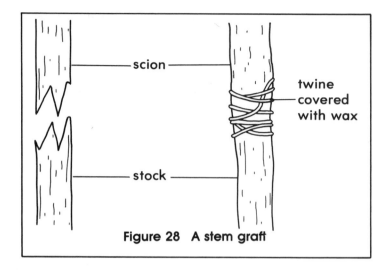

Figure 28 A stem graft

After about a month of growth, cut off the tomato stem below the graft, and the potato stem above the graft. Does the grafted plant produce tomato flowers and fruits? Does it produce potatoes?

• If you have access to an orchard (apple or pear, for example), perform a stem graft in which you attach a stem from one variety (for example, McIntosh apple) to a tree of another variety (for example, Rome Beauty apple). (Be sure to obtain permission before doing so.) Cut the stems with a sharp, clean knife **(caution!)** in such a way that they fit snugly and the cambium layers are in contact with each other. Fasten the two sections with raffia or twine and cover with grafting wax or paraffin. See Figure 28. What type of fruit will the upper branch (scion) produce? Why?

• Is it possible to graft a pear stem onto an apple tree? If so, what kind of fruit will the scion produce?

• Try to graft a stem of a plant from a different family, such as a grape, onto an apple or pear tree. Explain your results.

• Set up a living display of various examples of vegetative propagation. Include the following: leaf and stem cuttings in water; an onion bulb suspended in water that reaches up to its base; part of a potato tuber with an "eye," or bud, that has sprouted (if possible, obtain farm-fresh potatoes; the potatoes in supermarkets have probably been treated to prevent sprouting); the top 2- to 3-cm section of a carrot allowed to stand in a shallow pan of water; a rosette of pineapple leaves suspended over a jar of water; a sweet potato partially immersed in water; an example of grafting; and a strawberry plant runner. Type a short description of each on an identifying card. Use a title such as "Vegetative Propagation Produces Identical Plants."

TISSUE CULTURE

In tissue culture procedures, parts of a leaf, root, or stem are removed from a plant and grown to produce a genetically identical plant, or clone, on a nutrient culture medium in a glass container (petri dish, test tube, or flask). This growth must be carried out under aseptic conditions—conditions free of bacteria and molds. Special care has to be taken to sterilize the materials and handle them so carefully that bacteria and molds do not have a chance to be introduced. Do not become discouraged if your first trials become contaminated by these microorganisms. With a little practice, you can improve your techniques and obtain tissue culture clones. **Safety notes: Work under adult supervision. Wear safety goggles and a lab apron. Bleach has a strong odor, so avoid breathing the fumes and work in a well-ventilated area. If you spill any bleach on yourself, wash it off with water.**

Try a tissue culture project using African-violet plants. Start out by working in an area that has little or no air movement; avoid working near open windows or doors. Wash the area with water, wipe it down with paper towels, then wipe it again with a paper towel soaked in rubbing alcohol. Try to work with the materials well in front of you and do not lean over them. Store your instruments (twee-zers, scalpel, cork borer) in a solution of rubbing alcohol. Then, before you use them, drain off the excess alcohol so that they are quite dry. Holding the instrument with tongs, briefly and *carefully* pass it through the flame of a Bunsen burner or alcohol lamp. Allow it to cool for about 20 seconds before using it.

When you are ready to start, wash your hands and arms thoroughly for several minutes with hot water and soap. This may remind you of the "scrub" a surgeon goes through before entering a hospital operating room. The purpose is the same—to maintain a sterile environment. After rinsing, blot your skin with paper towels.

Prepare sterile 125-mL glass Erlenmeyer flasks of cul-ture medium plugged with nonabsorbent cotton. Violet culture medium can be obtained from a garden supply store or scientific supply company. Place 50 mL of the me-dium in each of six Erlenmeyer flasks and sterilize in a pres-sure cooker for 20 minutes at 250°F and 15 pounds per square inch of steam pressure. **A pressure cooker can be dangerous, so work closely with your supervisor.** Start timing after a steady stream of steam has become evi-dent, and then close the escape valve. At the end of the 20-minute period, allow the pressure to return to normal **slowly.**

Now that the conditions are right and the materials have been prepared, remove three healthy young leaves from the centers of African violet plants. Swab them with 95% ethanol. Then place them in a sterile petri dish and cover them with a 20% bleach solution for 10 minutes. Pre-pare the solution by placing 20 mL of bleach in a gradu-ated cylinder and adding water to the 100-mL level. Rinse the leaves three times with sterile distilled water.

Using a sterile #4 cork borer, punch out six disks from the central part of the leaves. Use sterile tweezers to trans-fer each to an Erlenmeyer flask. After you remove the cot-ton plug from the flask, *carefully* pass the mouth of the flask quickly through the flame of a Bunsen burner before

Figure 29 Plant tissue cultures
of tobacco plants showing
(a) callus formation, (b) callus
with roots and shoot, and
(c) the entire plant with flower.

inserting the leaf disk. Be sure the disk makes good contact with the surface of the culture medium. Set the flasks aside at room temperature (about 22°C) in indirect light, not in sunlight.

Keep a weekly record of the growth of the callus, the unorganized mass of plant cells that develops around each leaf disk within a month's time (Figure 29a). After about 1 to 2 more months, observe the growth of roots and shoots (Figure 29b). If all goes well, flower buds and flowers should develop after another 2 to 3 months (Figure 29c).

• Study the microscopic appearance of callus cells. Gently and carefully scrape a tiny section of the callus with a dissecting needle or scalpel onto a slide. Apply a stain such as methylene blue and add a coverslip. Use low power (100x) to examine the cells. Describe their appearance. Are they all alike? Why?

• Is it possible to grow the young African violet clone plants discussed above in small pots of soil when they are 3 to 5 cm high? Remove them carefully from the flasks and gently rinse under lukewarm water until any culture medium still attached is removed. Plant each clone in a separate pot. Cover each pot with a plastic bag. After a period of 7 to 10 days, open and remove the bag but do not let the plants dry out. Why are they considered clones? Compare them with the original plant.

• Try the tissue culture technique with other plants, such as tomato and petunia. Also, instead of using leaf disks, try a tiny section of a growing leaf tip.

• Instead of using kinetin to induce callus formation, experiment with coconut milk as a source of cytokinin (also known as kinetin). Add 100 to 150 mL to the culture medium before sterilizing it. (The procedure for preparing coconut milk is described at the end of Chapter 5.)

7

ECOLOGY

Plants can live successfully inside your home as long as you water them regularly, provide a source of light, and give them mineral fertilizer from time to time. Outside, in nature, however, plants live in relation to a complex environment that includes a combination of nonliving (abiotic) factors such as light, water, soil, pH, and temperature, and living (biotic) factors involving other living things. The study of this relationship of living things to each other and their environment is known as *ecology*.

One field of ecology involves the dependence of plants and animals on each other in the oxygen–carbon dioxide cycle. In an aquarium, fish give off carbon dioxide, which is taken in by plants when they carry on photosynthesis. The plants, in turn, give off oxygen, which is taken in by the fish. Another example is the nitrogen cycle, in which nitrogen is rotated between plants, animals, the soil, and the air, and in which nitrogen-fixing bacteria play a role.

In recent years, ecology has attracted much attention because of threats to the environment arising from pollution of the air, water, and soil. Plants as well as animals are the potential victims of such pollution.

• Conduct a project to illustrate the oxygen–carbon dioxide cycle. Anyone who has ever set up an aquarium knows that fish benefit from the presence of green plants in the water. What is the effect on fish if there are no plants present? Fill a 1-L battery jar or similar container two-thirds full of tap water. Let the water stand overnight in order to get rid of any chlorine it may contain. Add two small goldfish, each about 6 to 7 cm long, to the water. As a control, include a similar battery jar containing two similar goldfish and two 15-cm sprigs of the water plant elodea (also known as *Anacharis*), which you can obtain at an aquarium-supply store. Place the two jars next to a window but not in direct sunlight.

Feed the fish daily but sparingly, so that excess food does not contaminate the water. Observe the jars daily and record your observations. After 3 weeks or so, how do the fish in the two jars compare with one another? Account for any differences. Do you have to "rescue" the fish in the first jar? How would you do this? What do you conclude?

• Do the plants in the previous project benefit from the presence of the fish? Start with two 15-cm sprigs of elodea in a similar battery jar containing two small goldfish. Set up a control jar containing 15-cm elodea sprigs but no fish. Place the two jars next to a window but not in direct sunlight. Feed the fish in the first jar sparingly so that no excess food accumulates to contaminate the water. Keep a record of how much time it takes for the fish to eat the food. Add the same amount of food to the control jar and then remove it after it has remained in the water for the same length of time. Why is this step necessary?

At 2-week intervals, measure the length of the elodea sprigs in both jars. Prepare a graph to show their growth during the next 2 months. What do you observe and conclude from the graph?

Figure 30   Nodules on clover
roots contain nitrogen-fixing
bacteria (magnified × 12).

BENEFITS OF NITROGEN-FIXING BACTERIA

If you carefully dig up a clover plant growing on a lawn and gently wash the soil away from the roots, you should be able to see little swellings on the roots called nodules. See Figure 30. These nodules contain nitrogen-fixing bacteria *(Rhizobium)* helpful to the plant. They change the nitrogen of the air, which plants are not capable of using directly, into nitrates, which the plant needs to form proteins. Nitrogen-fixing bacteria play an important role in the nitrogen cycle.

The roots of members of the legume plant family, such as beans, peas, and alfalfa, also contain nodules of nitrogen-fixing bacteria. This useful relationship between legume plants and bacteria is an example of symbiosis, the intimate relationship between organisms of different species that live together. The form of symbiosis in which both individuals benefit from the relationship is known as mutualism.

Safety note: Wash your hands after working with soil and soil bacteria.

• Make a microscopic study of nitrogen-fixing bacteria. Carefully dig up a clover plant and gently wash away the adhering soil from the roots. Observe the nodules and remove a large one. Rinse it with water. **Exercise care** as you sterilize a scalpel and a pair of tweezers by quickly passing each through a flame and allowing it to cool. **Carefully** cut the nodule open with the sterile scalpel. Use the tweezers to smear the cut surface on a clean microscope slide that holds a small drop of water. Another way of obtaining a smear is to crush a nodule between two slides.

Allow the smear to dry. Hold the slide with forceps and "fix" the smear by carefully passing the slide quickly through a flame three times. Add methylene blue stain. After 1 minute, rinse the stain with water and allow it to dry in the air. Examine under the low power and high power of the microscope. Describe the size and shape of the nitrogen-fixing bacteria. See Figure 31.

• Prepare a display of the roots of various leguminous plants, showing their nodules. Carefully wash the adhering soil away and allow the roots attached to part of the stem to dry. Print the name of each plant on an appropriate label. Include pressed leaves of the plants. Also include a drawing or photomicrograph of nitrogen-fixing bacteria. Use a title such as "Nitrogen-Fixing Bacteria Live on the Roots of Legume Plants."

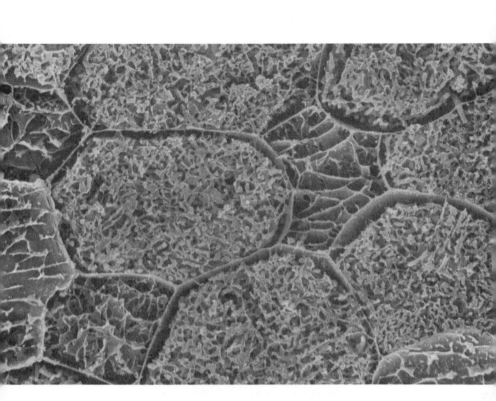

**Figure 31 Some of the cells in this
pea plant root nodule are filled
with nitrogen-fixing bacteria (the
spongy areas) (magnified × 1,000).**

• Do nitrogen-fixing bacteria help clover plants to
grow? Soak ten clover seeds overnight and germinate them
on wet towel paper in a glass container. When the roots
of the seedlings are 3 to 5 cm long, remove three of the
plants and soak the roots in a dense suspension of nitrogen-fixing bacteria for an hour.

This suspension can be prepared in the following way.
Carefully dig up several clover plants growing on a lawn
or in a field. Gently wash the soil from the roots to uncover
the nodules. Remove about thirty-five nodules and crush

them thoroughly in a small amount of water. Then add enough water to make a 75-mL suspension in a narrow container.

Plant the seedlings in individual pots of washed builder's sand. Similarly, set up three control plants whose roots were treated with ground-up nodules boiled for at least half an hour to kill their nitrogen-fixing bacteria, and then allowed to cool. Why is this step necessary?

Keep the plants next to a sunny window. As the stored food in the cotyledons is being used up, how do the plants begin to show differences in their growth? Of course, the lack of needed minerals in the sand will keep the plants from growing normally. However, does the presence of the nitrogen-fixing bacteria in the experimental plants make a difference? Record your observations. What do you conclude?

• Devise a project to determine whether nitrogen-fixing bacteria can take the place of nitrogen compounds in a hydroponic solution. Set up the following groups of clover plants:

Group 1, in complete nutrient solution;

Group 2, in nutrient solution that lacks nitrogen;

Group 3, in nutrient solution that lacks nitrogen but contains nitrogen-fixing bacteria.

SOIL pH

Various soils in which plants grow differ in their pH. The term *pH* refers to the degree of acidity or basicity of a substance. The pH scale extends from 0 to 14. A pH of 7 indicates a neutral solution. Pure water has a pH of 7. Below this, the lower the pH number, the stronger or more concentrated the acid; the closer the pH value approaches 7, the weaker or less concentrated the acid is. For examples: boric acid, 5.2; vinegar, 2.8; hydrochloric acid, 1.1.

Similarly, above pH 7, the higher the number, the more

basic the substance is. The nearer the pH value approaches 7, the weaker or less concentrated the base is. Examples: milk of magnesia, 10.5; ammonium hydroxide, 11.1; potassium hydroxide, 14.0.

Special indicators show the acidity or basicity of a substance. Litmus paper changes color from blue to red in acid, and from red to blue in base. Hydrion paper identifies a specific pH when used with a color chart. In addition, other special color indicators, as well as electric meters, measure pH.

Safety note: Wash your hands after working with soil.

• In what soil pH do different plants grow? Get permission to collect samples of soil from different locations in which a variety of plants are growing. For example, collect the soil from under a pine tree, pin oak, red maple, spruce, ailanthus, azalea bush, goldenrod, tomato, radish, cucumber, clover, blackberry, cosmos, and dandelion. Use a trowel to dig down 10 to 15 cm into the soil. Place small soil samples in separate plastic bags and label them with pieces of masking tape marked with the name of the plant.

Place strips of blue and red litmus paper about 5 mm apart on a small dish. Add about ½ teaspoonful of soil to the strips. Moisten the soil with water from a medicine dropper until the strips become wet. Brush the soil away and inspect the litmus papers. Is the soil acid or basic? Follow the same procedure with the other soil samples. Prepare a chart with the two headings "Acid" and "Basic," and make a list of each of the plants under the appropriate heading. Can you now predict whether a soil is acid or basic by looking at the type of plants growing there? Would you have to check your prediction? Why?

• Use Hydrion paper to determine the actual pH values of the soils in the previous project. Now list the plants in three columns according to the following pH distribution: pH 4–5; pH 6–7; pH 8–9.

Does pH affect the color of hydrangea flowers? Obtain three potted hydrangea plants of the same size. Water one with a solution of pH 4 and the other with a solution of pH 10. Solutions of pH 4 and 10 can be prepared by adding a buffer Hydrion pH capsule for each pH to separate jars containing 100 mL of distilled water. Make sure the pH in each solution is correct by testing it with Hydrion paper. As a control, use distilled water for the third plant. What is the color of the flowers that develop? Does hydrangea flower color depend on soil pH? What further steps should you take to confirm your answer?

ACID RAIN

In recent years, there has been much publicity about the harmful effects of acid rain on forests, lakes, and streams. See Figure 32. Acid rain is formed when nitrogen oxide and sulfur dioxide gases are given off into the atmosphere as wastes of fuel combustion by automobiles, factories, and power companies. When it rains, these pollutant products form nitric acid and sulfuric acid, which become part of the precipitation that falls to earth. There has been damage to plant and animal life because of the resulting increase in soil and water pH, especially in the northeastern United States. In some cases, the rain has been measured to be as acidic as vinegar.

• What is the pH of rainwater? If the carbon dioxide normally present in the air dissolves in falling rain to form carbonic acid, is the resulting rainwater slightly acidic? Collect rainwater during a mild rain and test it with Hydrion paper in the range of 5–6. What do you find? Is this considered acid rain? Why or why not? Compare with rainwater collected after a thunderstorm; after a steady rain lasting at least an hour.

• What is the effect of acid rain on the growth of geraniums? To represent acid rain with a range of acidity from mild to severe, prepare pH solutions of 5, 4, and 3

Figure 32   The effects of acid rain
on soybean seedling leaves have been
simulated in this photograph.

using buffer Hydrion capsules. Water each of four similar geranium plants with one of these solutions regularly. Use distilled water as a control on a fifth plant of the same size. What is the pH of this water? Keep a record of daily observations on the appearance of each plant. Is there a noticeable effect due to the different acid strengths? If so, how many days does it take for the effect first to be observed? Continue with your observations for twice this number of days. What do you conclude?

• Test the effect of "acid fog" on a geranium. Widespread acid fog in the Pacific Northwest has recently been found to be even more serious than acid rain because of the high concentration of fog droplets that "saturate" the plants. Using a plant mister or a spray bottle, spray the leaves of a geranium plant with a fine mist from a pH-3 solution every day for 2 weeks. Water the soil regularly with distilled water. Keep the plant covered with a bell jar. As a control, mist the leaves of a similar geranium with distilled water. Keep both plants next to each other on a windowsill, but not in direct sunlight. Make daily observations. You may wish to take photographs and prepare a display. What do you conclude?

• Devise a project to study the effect of acid rain (pH 3–5) on the development of nodules in various legumes, such as bush bean, soybean, clover. How are the nitrogen-fixing bacteria affected?

• How does acid rain affect the leaf ratio in radishes? Grow twelve pots of radishes. Separate them into three equal sets, A, B, and C, with each set containing four pots. Water set A with a solution of pH 3, set B with a solution of pH 4, and set C with a solution of pH 7. Four weeks after germination, measure the width and length, in millimeters, of at least six leaves on each plant. Calculate the leaf ratios by referring to this equation:

$$\frac{width}{length} = leaf\ ratio$$

TABLE 3. LEAF RATIO

Leaf Number	Width (mm)	Length (mm)	Leaf Ratio
1			
2			
3			
4			
5			
6			
Average			

Record the results for each of the pH concentrations in a table like Table 3. You will need four such tables for each set. (Do not write in this book.)

How do the average leaf ratios of the three sets of plants compare? What do you conclude?

• How does acid rain affect the growth of cuttings? *Carefully* use a sharp knife to cut off a 15-cm stem of a geranium plant. Dip the cut end in root hormone powder and then insert it in a pot of soil. Water the cutting with a solution of pH 4, representing acid rain. Set up a similar cutting as a control, and water it with distilled water. Measure the pH of the distilled water with Hydrion paper. After a month of growing the cuttings next to each other, compare their size and appearance. Remove them from the pots and gently wash the soil from their roots. Compare the length and appearance of the roots. Summarize the effects of acid rain on cuttings.

• Are cuttings of other plants similarly affected by acid rain? Try coleus, African violet, begonia, forsythia, and willow, for example.

• If you spend a summer vacation in the woods of the northeastern or northwestern United States, study the effects of acid rain on the trees and shrubs of the area. Use Hydrion paper to measure the pH of the soil and lake water. Notice such things as loss of leaves, change of leaf color, growth of seedlings, resistance to insects, and types of trees and shrubs affected. Take pictures and prepare a display entitled "Effects of Acid Rain." Include a map to show location and a brief statement of how acid rain is formed. Also, list your observations.

POLLUTION

When the pioneers first settled the United States, all the rivers were so clean you could drink their water without harmful effects. Today, this is hardly the case. Would you take a chance on drinking the water from a nearby river? Not only most rivers, but also the air and the soil, contain many pollutants. The Environmental Protection Agency (EPA) was set up by the government to prevent further harm to the environment and to suggest ways of cleaning up pollution that has already occurred.

One way of detecting chemically polluted water is the use of the simple *Allium* test, which makes use of the ordinary onion, *Allium cepa.* The test was first used fifty years ago to determine the effect of colchicine on the chromosomes in onion root cells. It is now used also to detect the effect of water pollutants on chromosome changes. Recently, the EPA sponsored a report describing the use of the method as a test for cancer-causing chemicals in humans. One advantage of the test is that results can be obtained in less than a week.

• Demonstrate the use of the *Allium* test. Start with at least twenty small white onion bulbs 1.5 to 2 cm in diameter. Other sizes may also be used, if necessary. Note that the onions purchased at a vegetable counter may not always be suitable because they have probably been treated with a growth inhibitor that prevents the onions from sprouting during storage.

Remove the loose outer scales of the onions and cut off a 1- to 2-mm slice from the base of each to expose the primary root cells. Prepare 0.5%, 1.0% and 1.5% solutions of sodium chloride. Expose five onions to each of the solutions by placing each bulb at the top of a test tube or small jar containing one of the solutions. Make sure the base of the bulb is in contact with the solution below it. The last group of five onions will serve as the controls and are to be exposed to distilled water.

Store the setups in the dark or in dim light at room temperature. Observe the water levels daily and add more liquid if necessary. In order to prevent contamination by bacteria or molds, it may be necessary to change the solutions daily.

You can vary this procedure by starting root growth of all the bulbs in distilled water. When the roots are 1 to 2 cm in length, expose them to the specific solution treatment. The advantage of this method is that you can replace any bulbs that did not sprout. It may require adding extra bulbs to your supply.

On the fifth day of the procedure, study one bulb at a time and use a millimeter ruler to measure the length of each of its roots. For greater accuracy, cut off each root as you measure it. Also note the following details for each bulb: number of roots; root-tip hardness; changes in root tip; bending of root; length of shoot. Summarize the total number of roots per bulb and the average root length per bulb.

Compare the results for each solution and the control. Account for differences. Compare with the results shown in Figure 33. What do you conclude?

• What effect does each of the above solutions have

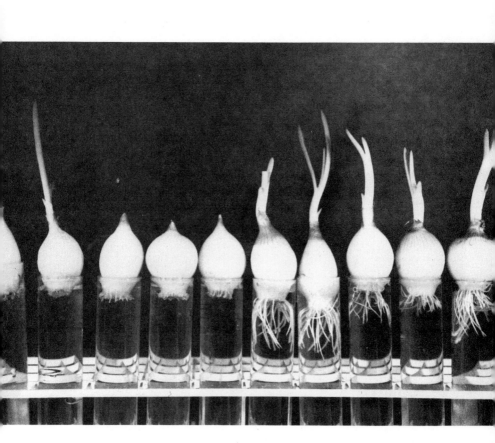

Figure 33 The *Allium* (onion) test is a simple way to test for the presence of polluted water. The five onions on the left were grown in polluted water; the onions on the right were grown in distilled water.

on the chromosomes of the onions? On the second day, remove one root from each solution and stain the dividing cells in the root tip according to the procedure described at the end of Chapter 3. Prepare a slide and examine it under the high power of a microscope. Observe 100 cells and count the number of cells undergoing active mitosis.

Calculate the mitotic index (MI), the number of cells undergoing mitosis per 100 cells:

$$MI = \frac{\text{number of mitotic cells}}{100}$$

To obtain more precise results, you may wish to repeat the procedure several times. Compare the MI of the experimental group with the MI of the controls. What are the results? What do you conclude?

• Conduct a project using the *Allium* test to study environmental pollution of any of the following: a river; a lake; contaminated soil in an industrial area; a farm where pesticides have been applied. Observe the effects on root growth and chromosome division or abnormalities.

• You may have read that the amount of carbon dioxide in the atmosphere has been increasing as a result of the burning of fossil fuels (coal, oil, and natural gas) by automobiles, factories, and homes.

Many scientists believe this increase will cause a "greenhouse effect" in which heat, which is given off when the earth warms up, is absorbed by the carbon dioxide in the atmosphere. Like the glass in a greenhouse, the carbon dioxide allows sunlight to pass through but does not allow the heat to pass back into space. It is thought that this greenhouse effect will cause the earth's atmosphere to warm up eventually, with harmful effects to the ecology.

Since green plants take in carbon dioxide during photosynthesis, could they possibly benefit from the added supply of the gas and show an increase in their growth? Devise a project to determine whether plants that receive an increased supply of carbon dioxide grow faster than those that don't. You may want to include the water plant elodea in your project.

8

OUT-OF-DOORS PROJECTS

Although most botany projects are conducted under controlled conditions indoors, many activities are also possible outside, under the open sky. Some places for such projects are garden, farm, forest, city, field, and marsh. All that is needed is curiosity about the natural world and ingenuity in pursuing scientific investigations.

Some out-of-doors projects have already been described in this book, in connection with specific plant activities. The following additional projects make use of the outdoors as a continuing laboratory for seeking answers to the ways in which plants live.

HOW AILANTHUS SEEDS SPREAD

The ailanthus is a common city tree that grows readily in backyards and vacant lots. It is often referred to as a weed among trees because it grows so freely in many different areas. It has even been found growing in such places as rooftops, the space under street gratings, and pavement cracks. Because of its widespread distribution, the ailanthus served as the inspiration for *A Tree Grows in Brooklyn,* a best-selling novel by Betty Smith.

How has the ailanthus managed to become so widely distributed? One answer lies in the structure of its winged seeds. Each seed is contained centrally in an elongated flat wing. Such a unit is called a *diaspore.* When the diaspore drops off the tree, it does not fall straight down to the ground. Instead, it can be carried by the wind for some distance from the tree.

To find out how diaspores may spread, collect at least fifty of them from an ailanthus tree and place them in a plastic bucket that has a removable lid. Press on the lid. Attach an eyebolt to the bottom of the bucket and another to the lid. Then attach a short length of rope to the bottom eyebolt and a longer piece to the lid eyebolt. Attach another piece of rope between the bolts so that the lid and bucket won't separate completely when the lid is pulled off.

Now attach the bottom rope to a flagpole rope (be sure to obtain permission). The flagpole should be located in an open area. In the absence of a flagpole, a rope could be suspended between two buildings or trees, and a rope could be thrown over the clothesline.

On a breeze day, hoist the bucket about 3 m up the flagpole. Now yank on the lid rope. When the lid is pulled off, the diaspores will be released and carried way by the wind. They will then settle to the ground some distance away. **Caution:** Avoid getting hit by the lid.

Measure the distance from the flagpole to the nearest diaspore. Then measure the distance to the farthest diaspore. Divide the area between into five equal zones and mark the boundary of each with a piece of wood. Collect the diaspores of each zone in a separate bag. Count the number of diaspores in the bags and list the results in a chart. Inspect the diaspores from each bag.

Do you see a relationship between their size and shape and the distance they traveled from the flagpole? Can you describe their type of motion as they fell to the ground? Repeat the activity several times and average the results for each zone. What conclusion do you reach about the shape and size of diaspores that travel the longest distances?

• Using quick-drying yellow spray paint, color code the diaspores that traveled the shortest distance. Similarly, use a different color, such as red, for diaspores that traveled the longest distance. Drop them again. The colors should make them easily distinguishable from each other after they have landed. Can you predict the results?

• Make a survey of places in the city where you can see ailanthus trees growing. Can you find any on a roof-top? Under a sidewalk grating? In pavement cracks? In a pile of dirt in the corner of a building? In a discarded barrel? Anywhere else that is unusual for tree growth? Take photographs and prepare a display.

• Since ailanthus is so hardy that it grows in places where few other trees can survive, can you design a project to determine the minimum amount of moisture its seeds need to germinate? The minimum amount of soil they need to germinate? The least nutritious type of soil that still permits germination?

• Prepare a display of winged seeds of trees that are dispersed by the wind. Besides ailanthus and maples, you might include elm, white ash, London plane, and linden.

• If you are ready for more advanced projects dealing with ailanthus diaspores, see the article "Wind Dispersal of Tree Seeds and Fruits," by James D. Thomson and Paul R. Neal, in *The American Biology Teacher*, November–December, 1989, Vol. 51, No. 8. There you will find additional ideas for such activities as adding weights to the diaspores, removing the seed portions, using a transparent millimeter grid to study dispersal, and applying statistical analysis.

HOW DANDELION SEEDS SPREAD

A homeowner who has conscientiously tended a lawn looks forward to being rewarded with an eye-pleasing thick turf of grass. However, from time to time, dandelions suddenly appear. With their flat rosette of leaves, yellow flowers, and white, gauzy seed clusters, they are thought to spoil the appearance of a nice grassy lawn. Where do these weeds come from and why do they appear so suddenly?

Plan a project to answer these and other questions about dandelion invasions. To start, locate some dandelions on a lawn or in a field. When you find a seed cluster (Figure 34), blow into it and notice how the weblike structures float away.

Look for another seed cluster. Study the arrangement of all the fine hairs that make it up. Use tweezers to gently remove one of the fine hairs. Do you see a seed attached to one end? Look at the other end. Can you tell why the collection of tufts there is called a parachute? (Note: The term seed is used here for simplicity. Botanically speaking, it and its parachute make up a type of dry fruit called an achene. The seed itself is contained within this tiny dry fruit.)

One by one, gently remove all the seeds, together with their parachutes. Count the number of seeds that are contained in the seed cluster. When all the seeds have been removed, study the receptacle to which they were attached. How deeply were they embedded? What evidence remains behind to show that the seeds were located there?

• Allow one dandelion seed to float away and follow it. How far does it travel before it comes down to the ground? Release other seeds, one by one, and follow each to its resting place. What happens to the parachute after a seed has landed on a lawn? Prepare a graph to show the distances traveled by the seeds of one seed cluster.

• Count the number of tufts contained in a dandelion parachute. Make a record of the number of tufts con-

Figure 34   The gauzy seed head
of a dandelion

tained in all the parachutes of a seed cluster. Do all the parachutes contain the same number of tufts? Compare the results in a study of five other seed clusters. What is your conclusion?

• Make a survey of the average number of tufts contained in dandelion seed clusters in an entirely different lawn or field.

• Determine the relationship between the number of tufts contained in a parachute and the average distance traveled by the seeds.

• Since dandelion is a weed that grows freely, can you predict the conditions necessary for its seeds to germinate? Place six seeds in a petri dish lined with moist filter paper. Keep it in a shaded place. How long do the seeds take to germinate? Compare with a similar petri dish kept in the refrigerator and with one kept in sunlight.

• Make a model of a seed cluster, using modeling clay, toothpicks, cotton thread, glue, and small beads. How does it compare with the real structure of a seed cluster?

COLLECTING MAPLE SYRUP

When the sap starts to flow in maple trees located in northern communities, around late February to mid-March, it is collected commercially to make maple syrup. It can also be collected for a maple syrup project. Begin as soon as the snow clears from around the trunks of maple trees. Select at least six sugar or black maples about 30 cm in diameter at chest height. *Be sure to obtain permission from the owner of the land, whether public or private.*

Commercial metal taps may be purchased at an agricultural supply store, or they may be made from metal pipes. **With adult help and wearing safety goggles,** drill a tap hole 5 to 8 cm deep using a $\frac{7}{16}$-inch bit and brace. Slant the opening slightly downward. Insert the tap into the hole and hammer it in lightly. For a larger tree, drill three tap holes spaced one-third the way around the trunk. Below each tap, hang a plastic bucket or an empty #10 can. **Watch out for sharp edges.** Drill a hole in the can just below the rim for the tap hook.

As soon as the sap starts to flow, collect about 4 L of it. Remove all the tap hooks but one, which you will need for further observation. Plug each hole with a wad of soft wax to prevent infestation by insects or fungi.

Strain the maple sap through cheesecloth into a large shallow pan and use a hot plate to slowly boil it. **Be careful if you have to use an extension cord—avoid getting it wet.** Work in a sheltered outdoor area that will not be damaged by the evaporating sticky vapors. The liquid will gradually become as thick as honey as it becomes maple syrup. Strain it into a jar through cheesecloth and cover tightly.

• Set up a display entitled "Making Maple Syrup." Include labeled examples of a tap, a bucket, a $7/16$-inch bit and brace, a covered bottle containing raw maple sap, a covered jar of homemade maple syrup, and a commercial brand of maple syrup. Also include photographs of maple trees fitted with taps and buckets, and a brief description of your procedure.

• Conduct a study of the flow rate of maple sap, using the remaining unplugged tap. For at least a week, make daily observations at regular intervals of at least 3 hours—for example, at 9 A.M. (or earlier), at noon, and at 3 P.M. (or later). Keep records of the following: amount of sap collected in a 3-minute period (use a graduated cylinder to replace the bucket temporarily); soil temperature; air temperature; position of tap (in sun or shade).

Is there a relationship between time of day and flow rate of sap? Does temperature play a role? What do you conclude?

• Conduct a project to measure the daily flow of sap over a 6-week period from February 1 to March 15. Prepare a graph and summarize your observations.

DAISIES IN THE FIELD

Locate a group of daisies growing in a field. Examine one of the flowers and notice that it is actually composed of many small flowers. The yellow center consists of a mass of disk flowers, and the white petals belong to the many ray flowers that grow around the center. In this respect, a daisy flower is really a bouquet of flowers, as you can see in Figure 35.

The daisy is a member of the aster family of flowers, all of which are composed of a multiple collection of small flowers. Examples of such flowers are aster, black-eyed Susan, dandelion, and goldenrod.

• Conduct a project to answer the question: How many petals does a daisy have? Carefully remove the petals of a flower head one by one and keep a count of the number. How many daisies should you include to reach a valid conclusion? Why? Tabulate your totals in a table and enter the results on a graph. What is your answer to the project question? Explain.

• How many disk flowers are there in a daisy head? How many daisies should you include in your count? Enter your results in a table and prepare a graph. Discuss your findings.

• Study the structure of disk and ray flowers. Remove a disk flower and observe it with a magnifying glass. How many of the following parts are there: stamens, pistils, stigmas, petals? Compare with the structure of a ray flower. How do disk and ray flowers differ from each other?

• Study the flower structure of other members of the aster family. How are they similar to a daisy? How do they differ?

PLANT LIFE IN A VACANT LOT

To city dwellers, a vacant lot is an empty lot. However, an investigation of such a lot will usually reveal numerous types of plants growing in abundance.

Figure 35   Why is a daisy
really a bouquet of flowers?

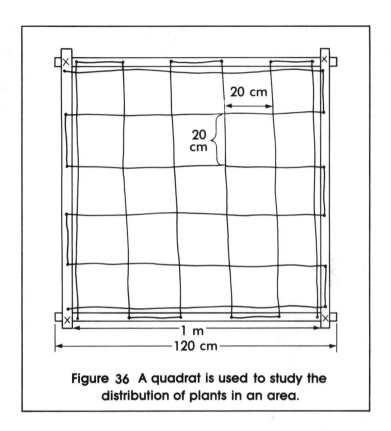

Figure 36 A quadrat is used to study the distribution of plants in an area.

• Investigate the different kinds of plants growing in a vacant lot. Use sample square areas to collect your information. Construct a grid, or quadrat, 1 meter square, made up of 20-cm squares. (See Figure 36.) Use narrow strips of wood, string, small nails, tacks, a hammer, and a meter stick for measurements. Be sure to obtain permission from your supervisor and from the lot owner.

To obtain representative information, place the quadrat on the ground in at least six different locations throughout the area. Tabulate the number of each type of plant in the squares, grouping them as grasses, herbaceous plants, or woody plants. Do any types of plants predominate? Do any types exist singly? To identify the plants, you may wish to refer to field guides of wildflowers, grasses, weeds, shrubs, and trees.

• Investigate other vacant lots for a study of their particular plant populations. Try to find lots in areas that have different characteristics (for example, sandy, moist, sunny, and hilly areas and areas overshadowed by tall trees).

• Look into the succession of plants in a newly cleared lot. Which are the first plants to start growing there? How many of each type are there? Keep a record, by date. At weekly intervals, make additional surveys of any new plant growth and continue with your record. As time goes on, is there a change in the number of the original types of plants? Do any particular plants appear to be dominant? Continue with your observations as long as possible. How has the picture changed, if at all, a year later?

IN THE GARDEN

Besides being a place for growing flowers and vegetables, a garden may also offer many opportunities for carrying on projects with plants. Some projects could deal with the effects of growing certain plants next to each other. Others could show the effects of chemicals or environmental conditions. Plant-breeding projects such as those suggested in Chapter 6 also present many other possibilities.

• Conduct a project to determine whether dwarf marigold plants planted next to tomato plants will protect the latter against insects. Compare with tomato plants grown in another section of the garden where there are no nearby marigolds.

• Devise a project to test a belief common among gardeners that citrus rinds can protect a rosebush against aphids.

• Borage plants are grown for their beautiful, bright blue, star-shaped flowers. When planted next to strawberry plants, the growth of both kinds of plants is supposed to be stimulated. Test this by growing borage and strawberry plants in rows 30 cm apart. Also grow another set of these plants a meter apart, and compare their productivity, in terms of size, number of flowers, and number of strawberries per plant. Note: It may be necessary to support borage plants with stakes against heavy winds and rain.

• Some plants give off chemicals that inhibit the growth of other plants. This effect, known as *allelopathy,* is a relatively recent discovery in the field of botany and one that could bear further research.

Conduct a project to investigate allelopathy. Start with sunflower plants in your garden. Carefully dig up their roots, wash away the soil, and grind them in the kitchen blender or with a mortar and pestle. To 10 g of the ground-up material add 100 mL of water. Filter the mass through cheesecloth and collect the filtered liquid (filtrate).

Water three young tomato plants with the filtrate. Compare the growth of these plants with controls given ordinary water. What to you observe and conclude?

• Grow tomato and sunflower plants next to each other. Compare their growth with that of similar plants growing far from each other. Record all observations and state your conclusion.

• Prepare sunflower filtrate and add it to a petri dish lined with paper toweling on which a dozen tomato seeds have been distributed. Set up a control dish treated with ordinary water. Store the two dishes next to each other. Keep a daily record of seed germination. Summarize your observations of germination rate. What do you conclude?

• Rhododendrons grow best in acid soil, pH 4.5–6.0. Irises do better at pH 6.0–8.0. What is the effect of planting irises alongside rhododendrons? Compare with the growth of irises next to a lilac or forsythia bush. Use Hydrion paper to determine the soil pH. What do you observe and conclude?

• How does soil acidity affect the color of hydrangea

flowers? Water the soil of three separated young hydrangea plants with pH solutions of 5, 4 and 3, respectively. You can prepare the solutions by adding a buffer Hydrion capsule for each pH to 100 mL of water. Keep a daily record of your observations. What do you conclude?

• Impatiens is popular as a garden plant because it flowers all summer long. Will it grow better in a heavily shaded part of the garden or in an area exposed to at least six hours of sunshine daily? Conduct a project to arrive at the answer.

APPENDIX:
SOURCES OF MATERIALS

Many types of plants may be obtained at a garden supply store or plant nursery. These places also often sell seeds, bulbs, plant hormones, chemical fertilizers, and special equipment for growing plants.

Additional materials can be obtained from companies that specialize in scientific supplies. Write to the Customer Service Department of any of the firms listed below, inquiring about the price and availability of materials you would like to purchase.

Carolina Biological
    Supply Co.
2700 York Avenue
Burlington, NC 27215

Connecticut Valley
    Biological Supply Co.
82 Valley Road,
P.O. Box 326
Southampton, MA 01073

Difco Laboratories
P.O. Box 1058A
Detroit, MI 40432
(agar preparations, tissue
    culture media, pre-
    mixed)

Fisher Scientific Co.
Educational Materials
    Division
4901 W. LeMoyne Street
Chicago, IL 60651

McKilligan Supply Corp.
435 Main Street
Johnson City, NY 13790

NASCO
901 Janesville Avenue
Fort Atkinson, WI 53538

Nutri-Sol Products
13240 Belcher Road
Largo, FL 34643
(Nutri-Sol for hydroponics)

Powell Laboratories
   Division of Carolina
   Biological Supply Co.
Gladstone, OR 97027

Science Kit and Boreal
   Labs
777 E. Park Drive
Towanda, NY 14150

Ward's Natural Science
   Establishment
5100 W. Henrietta Road,
   P.O. Box 92912
Rochester, NY 14692

Ward's Natural Science
   Establishment
11850 E. Florence Avenue
Santa Fe Springs, CA 90670

BIBLIOGRAPHY

Abramoff, Peter, and Robert G. Thomson. *Laboratory Outline in Biology IV.* San Francisco: W.H. Freeman, 1986.

Bartholomew, Rolland B., and Frank E. Crawley. *Science Laboratory Techniques.* Reading, Mass.: Addison-Wesley, 1980.

Beller, Joel. *Experimenting with Plants.* New York: Arco, 1985.

Biological Sciences Curriculum Studies. *Research Problems in Biology.* 3 vols. New York: Oxford University Press, 1976.

Bleifeld, Maurice. *Experimenting with a Microscope.* New York: Franklin Watts, 1988.

Carlone, Edward J. "A Sweet Springtime Adventure" (collecting maple syrup). *The American Biology Teacher,* February 1989.

Croall, Stephen. *Ecology for Beginners.* New York: Pantheon, 1982.

Darwin, Charles. *The Power of Movement in Plants.* (1882) New York: DaCapo Press, 1966.

Dean, Henry, and Robert W. Schuhmacher. *Biology of Plants: Laboratory Exercises.* Dubuque, Iowa: W.C. Brown, 1982.

Develin, Robert, and Francis Witham. *Plant Physiology.* Belmont, Calif.: Wadsworth, 1983.

Dodds, John H., and Lorin W. Roberts. *Experiments in Plant Tissue Culture.* Cambridge: Cambridge University Press, 1982.

Dowden, Anne O. *From Flower to Fruit.* New York: Crowell, 1984.

Eigst, O. *A cytological study of colchicine effects in the induction of polyploidy in plants.* National Academy of Science (U.S.) Proc. 1938, 24:56–63.

Englert, Karen M., and Nancy N. Shontz. "A Practical Method for Teaching Seed Stratification." *The American Biology Teacher,* March 1989.

Goodman, Harvey D., Thomas C. Emmel, Linda E. Graham, Frances M. Slaviczek, and Yaakov Shechter. *Biology.* New York: Harcourt Brace Jovanovich, 1986.

Hafner, Robert. "Fast Plants: Rapid-Cycling Brassicas." *The American Biology Teacher,* January 1990.

Hartmann, Hudson T., and Dale E. Kester. *Plant Propagation Principles and Practices.* Englewood Cliffs, N.J.: Prentice-Hall, 1990.

Kendler, Barry S., and Helen G. Koritz. "Using the Allium Test to Detect Environmental Pollutants." *The American Biology Teacher,* September 1990.

Klug, William S., and Michael R. Cummings. *Concepts of Genetics.* Columbus, Ohio: Merrill, 1986.

LaMotte Chemical Products Co. *The LaMotte Soil Handbook.* LaMotte Chemical Products Co., Box 329, Chestertown, Md. 21620 (Free copy available on request.)

Levan, A. "The effect of colchicine on root mitosis in Allium." *Heraditus,* 1938. 24:471–486.

Pietraface, William J. "Plant Regeneration" (tissue culture). *The American Biology Teacher,* April 1988.

Raven, Peter H., Ray F. Evert, and Susan E. Eichhorn. *Biology of Plants.* New York: Worth, 1987.

Ricklefs, Robert E. *Ecology.* New York: Chiron Press, 1990.

Salisbury, Frank B., and Cleon W. Ross. *Plant Physiology*. Belmont, Calif.: Wadsworth, 1985.

Science Service. *Thousands of Science Projects*. 1719 N Street, N.W., Washington, D.C. 20036. 1987.

Stegner, Robert W. *Plant Nutrient Studies*. LaMotte Chemical Products Co., Box 329, Chestertown, Md. 21620, 1971. (Free copy available on request.)

Stevens, William K. "Carbon Dioxide Rise May Alter Plant Life, Researchers Say." *The New York Times*, September 18, 1990.

Thomson, James D., and Paul R. Neal. "Wind Dispersal of Tree Seeds and Fruits." *The American Biology Teacher*. November/December 1989.

University of Wisconsin, Department of Plant Pathology. *Wisconsin Fast Plants*. 1630 Linden Drive, Madison, Wis. 53706. (Write for leaflets on Fast Plants.)

U.S. Department of Agriculture. *Seeds: Yearbook of Agriculture*. Washington, D.C., 1961.

Witham, Francis H., David F. Blaydes, and Robert Devlin. *Exercises in Plant Physiology*. Belmont, Calif.: Wadsworth, 1985.

INDEX

Acid rain, 114–118

African violet project, 103–106

Ailanthus seeds project, 122–124

Albinism, study of, 96

Allelopathy, 133

Allergies caused by pollen, 55, 74

Allium test experiments, 118–121

Anthers, 48, 50, 51, 52

Apple seeds project, 60–61

Artificial pollination, 52, 65

Autumn leaves project, 20

Auxins, 60, 82, 83, 84, 85–86

Botany projects:
choice of, 11–12
on ecology, 107–121
on flowers, 48–58
on heredity, 90–106
nature of, 9–11
out-of-doors, 122–134
on photosynthesis, 16–30
on plant structure, 31–47
on seed development, 59–89
writing reports on, 12–13

Brassica rapa project, 64–68

Bryophyllum project, 99
Buds, forcing, 38
Bud scale scars, 36–37

Carbohydrate, 21–23
Carbon dioxide, 16, 23–25,
    107, 108, 121
Carnivorous plants, 75, 79
Centrifugal motion, 76–78
Chlorophyll experiments,
    16–21
Chloroplasts, 21
Choosing a project, 11–12
Christmas cactus project,
    74
Chromosomes, 91
Chromotography experi-
    ments, 18–20
Clones, 92, 98–103
Clover plant project, 110–
    112
Codominance experiment,
    95
Coleoptiles, 83–84
Complete flowers, 49–50
Composite flowers, 50
Control, use of in
    experiments, 11
Corn plant project, 96
Cotyledons, 56–57, 58, 69,
    86
Cross-pollination, 52, 90–91,
    93–94
Cytokinins, 60, 82, 88

Daisies project, 129

Dandelion seeds project,
    125–127
Day-neutral plants, 73
Diaspores, 123–124
Dicotyledon, 56–57
Disk flowers, 50
Dispersal, seed and fruit,
    58, 123–127
DNA molecule, 91
Dominant traits, 90, 93
Dormant period in seeds,
    60

Ecology, 10, 107–121
Electromagnetic fields, 63–
    64
Elodea plant projects, 23–
    24, 28–30, 108
Embryos, seed, 56, 59, 63,
    65
Environmental hazards,
    107–108, 114–121
Environmental Protection
    Agency, 63
Epidermis, 33, 34
Ethylene, 82
Experimental projects, 10–
    11

Fast plants experiments,
    64–68
Fertilization, 55
Flower structures, 48–58
Foerster, Robert, 63
Food stored in seeds, 56,
    59

Fruits and seeds, 55–58, 60–64, 123–127

Garden projects, 132–134
Genes, 90–92
Geotropic response of seedlings, 78
Geranium plant projects, 22–23, 25–26, 116
Germination, seed, 60–64
Gibberellins, 60, 82, 86
Glucose, 16, 21
Grafting, 101–102
Grass flowers, 50–51
Grass seed project, 61–62
Gravity and plant growth, 76–78
"Greenhouse effect," 121
Growth and development, plant, 59–89

Heat and chloroplasts, 21
Heredity, 10, 90–106
Hilum, 56
Hormones, 82
Hybridization experiment, 95–96
Hydroponic experiments, 69–73, 112
Hydrotropism, 59–60, 75–76
Hypocotyl, 56, 59
Hypotheses, 10

Imperfect flowers, 50
Incomplete flowers, 50
Independent assortment process, 90

Insectivorous plants, 79
Insects, role of in pollination, 52

Lateral buds, 36, 82
Laws of probability, 92–93
Layering, 100
Leaf cuttings, 99
Leaf movements in plants, 79
Leaf scars, 36
Life Sciences Program, NASA, 72–73
Light and plant development, 21, 25–26, 62
Lima beans projects, 61, 68–72, 75–78, 79, 97–98
Long-day plants, 73, 82
Long Duration Exposure Facility satellite, 63
Longevity of seeds, 62

Maple syrup project, 127–128
Mendel, Gregor, 86, 88, 90–91, 93
Micropyle, 56
Microscopic studies, 10, 21, 34, 44–47, 52–53, 58, 65, 94–95
Microwave oven, use of, 32
Mineral requirements of plants, 68–73
Mitosis, 91
Monocotyledons, 57
Morning glory project, 95–96

Movement, plant, 74–81
Mutations, 91–92

NASA, 63, 78
NASA Seeds Project, 63
Nectar, 48, 52
Nitrogen-fixing bacteria, 107, 109–112
Nodules, 109–112

Onion bulb project, 44–47
Out-of-doors projects, 122–134
Ovaries, 48, 50, 85
Ovules, 48, 53, 65
Oxygen, 16, 28–30
Oxygen-carbon dioxide cycle, 107, 108

Paper chromotography, 18–19
Peas projects, 86–88, 92–95
Perianth, 50
Petals, 48
Photographic surveys, 44
Photoperiodism, 59, 73–74
Photosynthesis, 10, 16–30, 59
Phototropism, 59, 75
Pigments of chlorophyll, 18–20
Pistillate flowers, 50
Pistils, 48, 50, 51
Plant presses, 32
Plants, sexual reproduction of, 48–55

Plant structures, 31–47
Plumules, 56
Pollen, 51–55
Pollen tube, 53, 55
Pollination, 48–55, 65
Pollution, 119–121
Potato plant project, 101–102
Pressing leaves, 32

Radicle, 56, 59
Radish projects, 73–74, 116–117
Ragweed project, 74
Ray flowers, 50
Receptacle, 49
Recessive traits, 90, 93
Report writing, 12–13
Root systems, 40–47, 60

Safety precautions, 15, 18, 22, 23–24, 27, 32, 38, 35, 44, 58, 64, 65–66, 71, 72, 85, 86, 87, 88, 89, 95, 99, 101, 102, 103, 104, 110, 113, 123, 127, 128
Science fairs, 13
Seeds: Yearbook of Agriculture, 62
Seeds and fruits, 55–58, 60–64, 123–127
Segregation process, 90, 92, 93
Self-pollination, 51–52
Sepals, 49, 55
Short-day plants, 73

Sleep movements in plants, 79, 81
Smith, Betty, 123
Snapdragon project, 95
Soil, mineral content of, 69
Soil ph, 112–114
Space, exposure of seeds in, 62–63
Space Science Student Involvement Program, 78
Spectroscope, 27
Spinach project, 27–28
Stamens, 48, 50, 51, 52
Staminate flowers, 50
Starch, 21–23
Stem cuttings, 99–100, 117–118
Stems, 36–40, 60
Stigma, 48, 51, 52, 53, 55
Stomates, 33–36
Stratification experiments, 60–61
Style, 48, 53, 55

Tap roots, 41
Terminal buds, 36, 82
Testa, 56
Thigmomorphogenesis experiments, 78–79

Thomson, James D., 124
Tissue culture, 98, 103–106
Tomato projects, 62–63, 85–86, 101–102
Tree Grows in Brooklyn, A (Smith), 123
Tropism, 74

Ultraviolet light, 27
University of Wisconsin, 64

Vacant lot project, 129–132
Variation experiments, 96–98
Vascular bundles, 36, 101
Visible spectrum experiments, 26–28

Water and seed germination, 61–62
Went, F. W., 82, 84
Westinghouse Talent Search, 10
Williams, Paul W., 64
Wind pollination, 53

Xylem tubes, 39

Zero gravity, 79